The Naked Mystic

The Naked Mystic

James RQ Clark

Metanoia Press

The Naked Mystic. Copyright © 2021 by James RQ Clark.

All rights reserved. No part of this book may be reproduced in any form or by any electronic or mechanical means including information storage and retrieval systems, without permission in writing from the author. The only exception is by a reviewer, who may quote short excerpts in a review.

Cover Art & Design by Branka Jukic (www.brankajukic.com)

First Printing: April 2021
Printed in the United States of America

ISBN-13: 978-1-7336011-3-9

MetanoiaPress

Metanoia Press
www.metanoia.press

Dedication

For Jesus the Lion, the Amen who knows and tells the truth.

Table of Contents

Dedication 5
Prologue 11
Part 1: Assembly.. 13
Part 2: Purification 58
Part 3: Illumination 139
Part 4: Union..210
Part 5: Dismissal 263
Epilogue 291
Endnotes 293
Acknowledgements 311
About James R.Q. Clark.. 313

Who told you that you were naked?
(Genesis 3:11)

Prologue

I have believed
and people said
that I was a fool.

Now, somehow,
I know and find
that they were right.

Part 1: Assembly

And as he sat at dinner in Levi's house, many tax-collectors and sinners were also sitting with Jesus and his disciples—for there were many who followed him. When the scribes of the Pharisees saw that he was eating with sinners and tax-collectors, they said to his disciples, 'Why does he eat with tax-collectors and sinners?' When Jesus heard this, he said to them, 'Those who are well have no need of a physician, but those who are sick; I have come to call not the righteous but sinners.'

Mark 2:15-17

- 1 -

When did you become a Christian? he asked.

In my early twenties, I said. *That Night.*

It was a little like remembering a first kiss, except for the fact that it isn't really like that at all. Any analogy fades into insignificance here. It's trying to catch dragons with a butterfly net.

He was smiling.

Actually, that's not quite right, I corrected myself.

Oh? he asked.

It happened later. After That Night, I said.

My mind drifted back.

When I joined a church.

He nodded before asking, *And how long did it take before you realised that becoming anything was not going to help?*

I didn't have a ready-made answer to that one.

A long time, I said, after a long pause.

Too long.

- 2 -

It was our third meeting and the early stages of an extended conversation. We only ever talked about one thing, and that thing is not a thing.

Words, like the envoys of madness that they are, keep on doing the same thing here, over and over, expecting different results. It's a beautiful, unrequited love story that will never end. It's infuriating and inevitable. It is as it is.

Words rush in here, where the proverbial angels have always feared to tread. Then words run away from here, once they realise that they are in too deep and can no longer pretend to have any substance. In the end, words are happier when they are humble. When they know that they are empty.

Words don't need to stand alone then. They are allowed to fall back into the arms of the spaces between them. When words are seen to be translucent, the pauses leak through the pages and begin to suffuse our worlds with the speechless joy that the words were always looking for.

And that is why silence never feels the need to run away.

Silence is full.

- 3 -

He first appeared in the autumn.

I was walking my dog in the woods when I saw him walking slowly, ahead of us on the path. He was foraging for mushrooms.

It was September, and a spell of heavy rain had given way to a bright afternoon sun, which cooked the damp ground. The steamy, peaty scents hung in the air and made the world seem like a homelier place.

The weather down here does a lot. It's broody. The South-West is where a prevailing wind comes in off the sea, often pregnant with a rain that's been conceived over the Atlantic. It tends to affect the whole of the British Isles.

As we caught up to him and overtook him, I said, *Hello*.

He didn't answer.

I remember being offended and then wondered whether he was deaf.

Twenty or thirty paces later, I noticed that Philo wasn't with me anymore. I stopped and turned around to see the dog walking, to heel, next to him.

He never did that for me.

Part 1: Assembly

Here Philo, I called. *Come boy. Come here.*

It made no difference at all. Not even a flicker of acknowledgement. The dog just ambled, in time, at his heel.

As I waited and watched them approach, he smiled and said, *Nice dog.*

Thanks, I replied, as I turned and the three of us walked on.

Tea? he asked, after a few minutes.

Why not? I replied.

We turned the corner, and as the view opened out over farmland he pointed to an old cottage on the far side of a large paddock. It was backed by the familiar shape of the county's rolling hills.

I'm there, he said, pointing.

It was made from the local sandstone, which is the colour of honey. The thatch on the lee side of the roof was tinged with a deep, rich green. A thriving colony of moss.

Philo ran ahead and down the bridleway that led to the cottage.

What's your name? I asked.

Harvey, he replied.[1]

He didn't ask me for mine.

- 4 -

The second time we met was at his place.

I still don't really know what it was about him that took me back there. All I know is that on one grey, drizzly afternoon, I put a collar and lead on the dog, and we ended up at his cottage.

Fancy a walk? I asked when he opened the door to my knocking.

No, not really, he said. *I'm cooking.*

He turned his back on me before I had the chance to reply and said, *Come in.*

Philo headed straight for the warmth of his fireplace and curled up.

I'm in here, he called from his kitchen.

I walked in, took a seat at his table, and smiled at him.

I thought I might see you again, he said.

Really? I asked.

Yes, he answered. *I can always spot a heart in search of a home.*

I had no response to that. I suppose, looking back, that I always knew it was true.

- 5 -

Sometimes, and especially at his house while he was busy cooking, I'd watch him. He never seemed to notice.

I'd put him in his sixties, but he had the eyes of a child. The brightest blue, ringed with steely, silver-grey.

How old are you? I asked, once.

Not old enough to be your father, he said quickly.

Older brother, then? I countered.

That'll do, he laughed.

He was scruffy and seemed not to care much for his appearance. He looked like someone's mischievous uncle, but this ran alongside a kind of grace and elegance that was compelling.

I was a monk for a bit, he once declared.

It was a rare occasion of self-disclosure.

Why did you leave the monastery? I asked him. *Did they kick you out?*

No, he answered. *I found a door.*

He used a knife like a well-trained chef, but he had the hands of a farmer.

It led out of the cloister. So, one day, I opened it and walked.

It didn't make any sense, but somehow I could picture it. It was so vivid.

When he spoke again, it nudged me back to the present and to the kitchen table.

You might want to do the same thing, he said.

You look like a priest who can't live with his God anymore.

The statement floored me. I had no idea, at that stage, that he knew the slightest thing about me. It was as though he'd reached in and taken my heart by the throat.

And there's a door that will lead me out of here? I asked.

I didn't need explicitly to admit that he was right.

He was looking at me with curiosity. I was being examined. After a few moments he answered me.

Yes, there's a door. He was nodding. *But you might not want to step through it.*

Oh? I wasn't sure how to respond.

Admit that first and foremost you're a man who can't live with himself anymore, he continued.

The rest of it is just a story.

He was still watching me.

And even that is just a story.

He turned away and chuckled.

So many beautiful stories, he said to himself, shaking his head.

- 6 -

I should have known that I was never going to be able to play the priest.

On the night of my ordination, I had a dream. I was walking along a long corridor. Shafts of light pooled, here and there, on a flagstone floor from opaque, leaded windows on either side. There was a heavy, oak door up ahead, flanked by two sentries.

I'll take those from you, said one, as I approached.

He was pointing at my vestments: the stole I'd worn when the Bishop laid his hands on my head and the chasuble in which I'd presided over my first Eucharist only hours before.[2] I handed both over, without a word.

And I'll take the alb, said the other.

I pulled the hooded white robe over my head and put it into in his waiting hands.

You'll get them back on the other side, said the first sentry.

The second was nodding as I walked in through the door into what seemed to me to be an old vestry. The smell of incense and charcoal impregnating the walls and the woodwork was unmistakable.

The door closed behind me.

And it was dark.

- 7 -

A year after that day and that dream, I left parish ministry. I just wasn't suitable. It's a wonder that I ever thought I would be.

It's difficult to describe why. Perhaps the priestly persona was a burden too heavy to bear. Or, maybe, I was struggling with the reality of parish life and discovering that there were far more pressing agendas than God and the care of souls competing with each other for prominence.

Whatever the reasons, small cracks turned into big cracks and the dream shattered.

And so, I found myself heading for my long-empty family home in the South-West of England. Late summer gorse-blossom flanked long stretches of the ancient road that has taken travellers from London to Exeter, via Stonehenge, for what might be thousands of years. Some say the flowers smell of coconut. I can't smell it.

I had been honest with the Bishop but that presented him with a problem: I had been a very popular priest and the parish was shocked to hear that I would be leaving so soon. They had taken me to their hearts.

I can't do this any longer, I said.

He smiled, initially.

It always takes time to settle into a priesthood, he assured me. *It's not a natural fit for anyone, really.*

My newly ordained colleagues seemed to be thriving. I pointed that out.

Just give them time, he said. *It comes to us all.*

It was a painful conversation that went on for a lot longer than I care to remember.

The Bishop was a good man who had been good to me. I was acutely aware that I was letting him down. He had placed a fatherly confidence in me, and my decision, as well as disappointing him, shook his confidence in his own judgement.

Where will you go? he asked when he finally accepted that I couldn't be persuaded.

Home, I replied.

The key was under the doormat. I sold the car and adopted a dog. I opted for a large, lazy-looking, brindle lurcher.

I called him Philo because the Sufis often call God 'the Friend' and I needed one.

- 8 -

You mentioned That Night, Harvey said. *What happened?*

God made an appearance, I replied.

I cast my mind back.

I was alone, in bed, and suddenly God was in the room.

It's a story I had told before and I always felt awkward doing so. It doesn't invite embellishment. It's too bald.

I can't put it any better than that.

He was listening, intently.

It was all real. There he was. Terrifying and utterly compelling all at the same time.

How old were you? he asked.

In my early twenties.

It seemed like yesterday but, in reality, something like thirty years had passed between That Night and this conversation.

And that changed everything? he asked.

Yes. I was lost and alone without knowing it, and then, suddenly, I wasn't.

The memory brought back a deep thrill and a yearning that has never left me.

On That Night, it was as though the Spirit hovered over the waters of my chaotic, empty existence, and then there was life and love.

It was unforgettable.

Until then, I had been a shadow, nothing more.

But you are lost and alone now, he said.

I had to laugh.

Yes, I said. *I suppose I am.*

What's different because of That Night, then? he asked.

It was a good question.

It was late afternoon, and we were walking along the banks of the river that ran through the water-meadows on the south side of the town. Dog walkers and their charges peppered the grassy fields here and there. It was a popular spot.

It's a different kind of lostness, I said. *A different loneliness. Back then I didn't even know that I was just a shadow.*

So, the only difference is that you were blind but now you see? he asked.

Yes, I said. *Something like that.*

But there's more, I added. *There's something else here. There's a kind of company in this seeing.*

He smiled and nodded.

As we walked on and towards the stile, Philo fell in beside me and I slipped the lead on him.

Who's doing this seeing? he asked.

Me, I said. *But also, not me.*

I was floundering.

What do you think? I asked. *Is it you that sees this?*

I can't tell you that, he said.

He stepped over the fence and lifted the dog gate for Philo.

Part 1: Assembly

I'm gone, he said. *Long gone.*

And with that I lost sight of him.

The dog ambled happily next to me, and as I walked home, past the station and cutting through Pavilion Gardens, the streetlights gently flickered to life. As I got to Forge Lane and my front door, the rain was coming down, steadily.

- 9 -

My house was a lonely, empty place for the best part of that year. I barely furnished it. I slept on a single mattress on the floor.

I don't know that I would have survived it without the love of the dog.

Hey boy, I'd say to him, *do you know what's going on?*

He'd look at me and cock his head to the side when I spoke like this.

At night, when it was very cold, he'd crawl under my blankets.

Hey boy, I'd ask, *are you as lost as I am?*

Occasionally he'd head for the door if my tone was more cheerful. He thought that kind of talk signalled a walk.

I woke every morning well before dawn, made coffee and smoked in the garden. On cold mornings I'd wrap up.

Hey boy, what goes on in that head of yours?

Then I'd walk around the town as the shopkeepers set up for the day. The butcher often waited for the dog and he was always obliged with affection in exchange for a handful of offcuts.

By the time the town stirred I was back at home.

I'd often head to Harvey's in the late morning, afternoon, or evenings.

Hey boy, want to go for a walk?

And through it all was God. A troubling, searching mystery that unravelled me and gripped me more deeply every day. But I can't really put that into words.

All I know is that God can love and reassure a man through the loyalty and friendship of a dog.

Hey boy, come here.

And that God can heal a man through the ministrations of another man. A man I came to depend on and trust but never really understood.

He often seemed to be at home when I knocked, and it always puzzled me that, even though we were in a small town, I never ran into him or bumped into him.

I thought I saw him once, from the back, but it wasn't him.

- 10 -

The next time I saw him we went walking again and he wasted no time in dragging me back to the memories of That Night and my conversion.

And after That Night? he asked. *What then?*

A new heaven and a new earth, I said.

I cast my mind back.

All was love. Nothing but love and light and warmth.

Thinking about it always makes my heart purr.

Like coming home and finding out it's the place my heart has always longed for, even though I did a good job looking everywhere else.

As we walked, he ran his right hand along the top of a long privet hedge.

I knew everything, I said.

Everything? he asked.

Well, yes, I replied. *I saw that love was everything and that it was everything that anyone had ever wanted.*

It was so clear.

And that everything is a search for love. However misguided and perverse.

Perhaps the more misguided and perverse the attempt the greater the desperation? It was more of a statement than a question.

That makes sense, I answered.

As we walked past a row of rosemary planted along the length of a garden wall, he plucked some leaves and rubbed them, hard, between the palms of his hands.

That's all sin is you know.

What? I asked.

Looking for love in all the wrong places, he said.

He had his hands cupped over his nose and he was breathing in the scent of the crushed rosemary.

Tragic, he said.

We walked on and he asked, *So what happened? How did you lose it?*

I had to think about that for a while.

I didn't know who to talk to, I said, eventually. *So, I drifted.*

My life changed forever on That Night and, as I walked around looking at a new world through new eyes, I didn't know that it would take me the best part of the next thirty years to begin to understand what had actually happened.

The Bible goes some of the way to describing the sense of well-being and security that filled and surrounded me for a few months after That Night. Some verses from Psalm 91 come to mind: "You who live in the shelter of the Most High, who abide in the shadow of the Almighty, will say to the Lord, 'My refuge and my fortress; my God, in whom I trust.'"

What I know now is that there's a world of difference between Ecstatic Union and Habitual Union.[3]

Any idiot can have a religious experience, Harvey said. *But it takes an idiot with courage to run the narrow gate and walk the hard road.*

The experience is just a promise, he continued. *It's a pledge. A hint. Nothing more.*

Don't set up shop around your experiences.

- 11 -

I hadn't yet worked out that I was sitting in the dark vestry of my dream after ordination, and I certainly never imagined I would be there for quite as long as I was.

My spiritual life, a source of comfort and direction to me for the last thirty years or so, was offering no assurances. I was lost. I couldn't see. It was night and I was trying to resist it.

God, help! I don't know what to do.

It was my constant and only prayer and it erupted from deep within, again and again.

I was saddled with a constant and nagging conviction that I needed to do something to bring this painful episode to an end. At the very least, something needed to happen, whether I was the agent of that event or not.

Harvey was no help at all.

Tell me about your spiritual practices, I asked.

There aren't any, he replied, with a shrug.

So, what would you say to anyone seeking Union?

Nothing, he answered.

He could be exasperating at times but often, when I thought he was being deliberately obtuse, he would take an unexpected turn.

They are all methods for coping with emptiness and pain, that is all, he continued.

Oh?

And they don't work, he said.

Tell me about your methods for coping with emptiness and pain, then? I asked.

This made him smile briefly.

I played ten thousand games of Solitaire, he said.

- 12 -

I was in search of a ladder. In my desperation, any spiritual practice that promised to lift me out of the disorientated space in which I found myself would have done.

I wasn't looking for Union. I was looking for relief and he knew it before I admitted it to myself.

Why do you come here to see me? he asked.

After what I hoped looked like a thoughtful pause, I answered, *Because I want to get closer to God.*

He chuckled.

That implies that you've found him; we get closer to something we know is there.

It was true, but it seemed like a smug and cheap observation.

As I wondered what I was really doing at his place, he asked again, *Why do you come here?*

I'm not sure.

He pressed on. *What do you imagine getting closer to God will do for you?*

Well, I hope it will make me happier...

His laughter cut me off.

So, you're here because you're unhappy? What makes you think you're unhappy?

I'm in pain, I said.

He nodded, without sentiment. *And you think getting closer to God will take your pain away?*

Well, now that you put it like that, I'm not really sure.

So why are you here? he asked, again.

There was no irritation in his voice. It wasn't in the least patronising and it wasn't a rhetorical question.

I don't know. I just am.

I still don't know why I kept going back to see him.

- 13 -

When autumn comes, I can always feel it in my feet first, which is why I am convinced that autumn rises. It ascends from deep in the earth somewhere to spread upwards into the trees and choke them until they are starved and can no longer feed their leaves.

It's as though the retreating sun acts like a counterweight and pulls the autumn from the depths of its damp, sombre lair.

It's a glacial creep that, in time, languishes into winter.

It was mid-October, and we were walking in the woods. The leaves were thickening on the ground.

I keep asking you why you come to see me, he said. *Don't you ever wonder why?*

I haven't really thought about it, I said. *I suppose you are asking because you want me to see something.*

There was a sweet, peaty smell in the air and shafts of sunlight pierced through here and there.

Death follows birth as surely as night follows day. What makes you think you will be born again without dying first? he asked.

I didn't answer.

You come to die, he said, as we paced in time.

We turned a corner and the view over the vale opened up before us.

You long for an end to the charade you call You.

Yes, I replied. *I do.*

We stood, scanning the landscape to the west. There were a few hay bales remaining but otherwise the fields had been stripped of their summer crops.

Tell me about the death you're talking about? I asked.

He smiled. It was as though this was what he wanted to talk about the most.

It's the end of everything and the beginning of everything, he replied.

The Alpha and the Omega? I asked.

I was hoping to find my coordinates with metaphors I could relate to.

Nice touch, Reverend, he said, dryly.

How does it come? I pressed.

Nobody can really say, he answered. *It blows where it pleases, and we don't know where it comes from or where it goes.*

That's unhelpful, I said.

Really? he asked. *I was only quoting the Bible you seem so fond of.*

I hated the mounting vulnerability that often made an appearance when I was with him.

You want help dying? he teased.

After a moment, he said, *OK. Lectio Divina three times a day, Centering Prayer and a Daniel Fast.*[4]

And you could also light some incense and listen to vegetarian music, he said. *That'll finish you off.*

He was chuckling to himself when I turned to him and said, *You're not serious.*

Of course not! he cried. *After a while, that stuff is not at all helpful. It will keep you half alive forever.*

The afternoon sun was low in the sky and we backtracked.

It's spiritual life support and you ought to turn it off while you can.

- 14 -

By the time we were back at his place it was dark. He lit a fire and asked me to make tea.

Why did you say that spiritual practices are not helpful after a while?

I wondered if you would pick up on that, he said. *They are worse than unhelpful.*

Can you say why? I asked.

It's hard to explain, he said, *like many things.*

He stopped talking for a while. When he did give me an answer of sorts, he was watching my face intently.

The I Am is content to be naked, he said. *Why dress it up?*

But some practices aren't just play-acting? Surely?

They are all just play-acting, he replied. *We just don't see it for a while, so I suppose it depends on the practice and the timing.*

I thought of the hours I had spent engaged in some sort of spiritual activity.

They keep the Phantom alive, he said.[5]

Actually, it's worse than that. They give the Phantom phylacteries to wear.[6]

- 15 -

I was stuck.

My strategies for propelling myself into a future I liked the look of were fading fast and the intolerable reality of my inadequacy to the task was beginning to settle in.

It's the simplest thing in the world, to do nothing. It's also the most difficult.

We had planned to meet at the pub at seven. He was late.

There's something about waiting for someone that brings out the worst in me.

There's nothing for you to do now, he said, once he'd ordered his pint and joined me at our usual table. *Nothing at all.*

Just waiting? I asked.

That's it, he said. *That's all of it.*

Contemplation is an old Christian word for meditation. That's a shorthand definition but it serves well enough. It's a search for the presence of God and for the fullness of God, as far as that is possible in this mortal coil.

The great mystics wrote at length about the transition from active to passive contemplation. They also said plenty about how painful that transition can be.

There's a point at which our own efforts, our practices and disciplines, and even our convictions, are overridden by the activity of the Holy Spirit. At this stage, all effort is useless.

There comes a time when all we can do is wait on the will of another.

You hand yourself over, he continued. *That's all.*

I cast my mind back to an Anglican theologian I had wrestled with years before. It was rare that any of my reading came in handy these days, but it was then that I remembered W. H. Vanstone, who first taught me, long before I was ready to realise the truth of it, that the opposite of action is passion.[7]

It's where a painful, naked kind of helplessness is transmuted into patience and patience is transmuted into trust.

Trust is what faith is.

Behold the handmaid of the Lord, I said. *Be it unto me according to thy word.*

Thanks, he replied as he slid his glass across the table towards me, *I'll have another.*

He winked.

Same again.

- 16 -

You seem a little lost today, he said as we walked.

Philo was running here and there, preoccupied with the scent of rabbits.

Yes, I said. *I am.*

It was early November. The day was warm for late autumn, and the morning was damp.

My mum used to sing a hymn on good days: It Is Well With My Soul.[8] *Know it?*

No, he answered. *Not off the top of my head.*

We walked on a bit before he asked, *And it's not well with yours?*

No, I answered. *Not at all.*

Philo was digging at the entrance to a burrow when we caught up to him. He turned to look at us, muzzle covered with fine, rich soil.

But it was yesterday? he asked. *Your soul was well yesterday?*

It seemed to be, I said. *But today it's as though I don't even have one. God is like an enemy.*

He gave Philo a pat on his back as we walked past him and said, *They're like feathers on a wind, you know?*

What are? I asked.

Our souls, he answered.

There was a reassuring tone to him.

When the wind is up it's all we can feel, and we lose sight of the feather.

I was troubled by that. How does a person function when their grasp on a self is so tenuous that the wind seems more stable than their very own self?

There's something wrong, I pressed. *And I can't find out what it is.*

Looking back, it's all so obvious: Job's Comforters. The conviction that when all is not well, a hidden sin is at the heart of the whirlwind. If it can be found and rooted out, scapegoated, and driven into the wilderness, the peace and sense of favour that rests on a life can be restored.

I was looking for anything. I would have confessed to everything.

Sounds like you want a confessor, he said. *Why?*

I'm not quite sure, I answered. *There are things I can't seem to shift.*

Oh? he said. *Sounds like another spiritual strategy.*

You can't just yank on a confession lever to pull yourself out of this, you know?

Humour me? I asked.

OK, he replied. *Things you can't stop thinking or doing, or things you feel you are?*

I had to think for a while.

Both, I said.

He was waiting for more.

I don't know how to put it, but I feel...

I tailed off, looking for the right word.

...wrong.

Wrong? he asked.

Yes, but it's more than that, I said. *Maybe even bad, or depraved.*

That's good, he nodded. *We all have to live with those for a while.*

It was surprisingly easy to talk to him.

And the things you're thinking and doing, he said, *don't worry about those either.*

Don't worry? I asked.

Yes, don't worry, he replied.

They'll die when they stop being useful to you.

- 17 -

He made it all sound like the simplest thing in the world. It wasn't.

By now I was beginning to struggle with a rising tide of anger, helplessness, and despair. He seemed happy to let me drown, without the slightest suggestion that anything could be done about it.

In my increasing distress I clung, ever tighter, to my so-called Christian faith. It can only ever be an interpretation, of course, but that's all I ever had, if I am honest.

It was a house built on sand, erected to protect myself from a reality I couldn't cope with. My life's work consisted of keeping that structure, that temple, intact, and building on it with new interpretations when they became evident and available.

It was my hidden vocation. I called that progress. I called it growth.

I wasn't about to acknowledge it, but it was time for the house I'd been building for so long to collapse. Time the rain fell, and the floods came, and the winds blew and beat against that house.

He was, as always, well ahead of me.

- 18 -

We were in his garden. The autumn was tailing off into the quiet hush of winter and the last of the autumn sunshine bathed us.

The dog was smiling, asleep in the sun and breathing in the crisp, cold air.

So, what have you been doing all this time?

I'm no longer sure, I answered.

There were vegetable and flower beds running along both sides of a long, narrow deck. Fruit trees were scattered here and there around the garden but nothing else was cultivated at all. It looked more like an allotment than a garden.

What did you think you were up to? he asked.

I thought I was looking for God, I replied.

But you discovered that you weren't? he enquired.

Yes. I replied. *I was really looking to become a saint. It's very different, I think.*

He started to laugh then. It bubbled up in him and overflowed like running water.

I remember that, he said. *I spent years running that same, futile race.*

Mind if I smoke? I asked.

No, he said.

I lit a cigarette and inhaled deeply.

Finding God doesn't make you a saint, he said.

No, I said, shaking my head.

So, he asked, *are you ready to be sick for a while?*

Yes, I said. *I think so.*

- 19 -

Later, as the light began to fade and the cold began to bite, we smoked a cigar each. We were drinking his home-brew.

Were there any important milestones for you? I asked.

He thought for a while before saying, *Yes. Quite a few.*

Any that might be helpful to me?

We were wrapped in old, grey military blankets. He had a stock of them from somewhere.

Well, he said, *there was the time I realised that George Fox was talking to me.*

The Quaker?

Yes, he nodded.

He was looking for God as a young man, and after doing the rounds of all the clergy he could find, he said that he came to the conclusion that they 'did not possess what they professed.'[9]

And you realised that was you? I asked.

Yes, he replied, quite casually.

After another puff on his cigar, he added, *One of the priests he spoke to advised him to take up tobacco.*

I laughed. It couldn't have been stage-managed any better.

How about you? he asked after a brief silence.

How about me?

Yes, he said. *Do you possess what you profess?*

I couldn't answer that.

- 20 -

As the fire burned low and I sensed that the day and the evening were drawing to a close, I pressed him on his own religious life. I was hoping to drag things out because I didn't want to go home, but that wasn't the main reason.

I was getting to the point where I no longer believed I would uncover any spiritual resources in my own psyche, so I was looking for some in his.

It's a common spiritual practice: looking for one's own path and salvation in the lives of others. I had read countless biographies and autobiographies. As though a description can ever be a prescription.

What was your biggest failing?

Cowardice, he answered, without the slightest hesitation.

I didn't respond immediately even though I wanted to know more.

I couldn't tell them the truth, he continued.

What truth?

God is a thief, he said.

A thief? I wasn't sure that I'd heard him right.

Yes, a thief. A plunderer, he continued. There was a fire in his eyes as he spoke.

So, I couldn't bring myself to tell them that their citadels would be razed to the ground and that their altars would be laid to waste.

I knew he was borrowing from the Book of Lamentations, but I had no idea what he was talking about.

And I also lacked eloquence, he said.

How do you mean?

After a moment where he looked as though he was searching for words, a sad, slightly defeated smile came over his face and he said, *I couldn't find the words to express to them the bliss of poverty.*

Yes, he muttered, nodding to himself. *That's it.*

I wasn't sure what he meant, at all. 'Blessed are the poor' was never something I related to, let alone understood.

He turned then and looked at me directly. *I'm struggling now*, he said.

Struggling with what? I asked. I was feeling very uncomfortable.

Struggling to get you to face your poverty, he replied. *Struggling to get you to stop trying to tunnel out of it. Struggling to get you to see the beauty of bankruptcy.*

In that moment, he looked something like a baby's laugh.

- 21 -

I ended up getting myself into trouble, I said.

Trouble? he asked.

Yes.

I wandered the new earth and, after the euphoria of That Night had dimmed and daily life and the business of earning a living stretched out before me, there were things I found too difficult to resist.

Don't they call that back-sliding? he asked.

Yes, that's it, I answered. *I don't understand why I did that.*

It still surprises you? he asked. *After everything you have come to learn about yourself recently?*

It's not really surprising any more, I said. *Maybe disappointing is the right word.*

Part 1: Assembly

I had been enveloped and invaded with a love I couldn't even begin to put into words, and, like the proverbial Prodigal Son, I had squandered my inheritance on sex, drugs, and rock and roll.[10]

We were walking Philo through the town. It was a crisp, sunny, late-November day.

You still had a lot to learn, he said, simply.

Maybe, I answered.

When did you realise you had bankrupted yourself? he asked.

I wasn't sure I understood what he meant by that.

Well, it happened literally when I spent the last of my money on a good bottle of vodka.

Was the vodka good enough to be worth it? he asked with a smile on his face.

I laughed.

It was my birthday and I had drunk it alone.

No, I said. *Not really.*

We walked in silence and I was filled with a deep, melancholic sense of regret.

I don't even remember how I got there but I woke up the next morning in a stranger's bed.

He nodded.

She wasn't the first.

He was listening carefully.

And she was beautiful.

I remembered her face.

Beautiful and lost. And I had nothing to give her.

I could almost taste the melancholy.

It was the loneliest, saddest moment of my life.

And that's when you decided to come home? he asked.

Yes, I said.

That was the exact moment.

- 22 -

There's a spiritual practice called Journaling. I had given it a go over the thirty or so years that I had attempted to live the Christian life. It's writing down your dreams, insights, thoughts, and feelings for the purposes of self-analysis and self-discovery.

It's a reflective practice and a practice of discernment. The idea is to pick up traces of the divine in your life story. It's looking for God's tracks.

I was still practicing a form of it, I suppose, because I wrote poetry. It was a way of trying to capture something I couldn't understand.

So, I showed him this one.

> That church – you know the one – on the hill
> fed me their Jesus, for a while back there,
> and even promised that he would follow me,
> until I would swear, half-blind and crazed,
> that I could taste him always and everywhere.
>
> So, I limped and crawled for years, because
> that Jesus wasn't allowed to point at cripples.
> His thin, cheap blood was like the altar wine,
> a chalice that was far too easy to suckle from.
> It made a baby – a fat, floating syrup of me.
>
> That muzzled Jesus couldn't mend these
> arms and legs, these shaking, twisted hands
> – they needed to be seen and broken first.
> Angry that I fumbled for him in my own
> pockets, he watched me, silent and fuming.
>
> Then one day I heard him say, Ask me!
> Ask me for courage and nettles and pine,
> and strong winds and rough pumice. Ask!

> So, I did, and he came, dressed in a storm
> with which to tear the grave-clothes off me.

What do you want me to say about it? he asked.

He was frowning.

I'm not sure, I answered.

His response had startled me.

Well, I can't say it's any good, he said. *And that's being polite.*

I reached out and took the poem from his hand.

He was looking at me.

What do you want me to see? he asked.

It's a snapshot of where I am at, I suppose, I stammered.

You're the fat, broken baby? he asked. *And you're hoping that I'm the nettles and strong winds and rough pumice?*

I didn't know what to say.

Or are you hoping that I'll tell you what a spiritual hero you are?

He paused.

As though my buying that story would make it true?

I just showed you a fucking poem. That's all, I protested.

He laughed.

No, he said. *I don't think you showed me a poem. I think what you did was show me an advert.*

My embarrassment was turning to anger.

You're selling me your glorious, spiritual self, he added.

And you're an obnoxious prick, I snapped.

I had had enough of him for that day.

As I turned to leave, he said, *I knew it.*

Knew what? I growled.

One touch from the nettles and pine and you're off? What will you do when the strong winds and rough pumice come?

As I walked out, he said, *Your advert is misleading. You're not what you say you are at all.*

He was right.

I had, for a long time, admired a passage by Thomas Merton, who makes Harvey's point in more elaborate prose: "The logic of worldly success rests on a fallacy: the strange error that our perfection depends on the thoughts and opinions and applause of other men! A weird life it is, indeed, to be living always in somebody else's imagination, as if that were the only place in which one could at last become real!"[11]

What I hadn't done was taken Merton's lines and applied them to myself. Harvey drove my hypocrisy home.

It was painful, but I had nobody else to talk to.

- 23 -

At the end of November, I dreamt about my old Bishop.

He was walking down the corridor of my earlier dream in which I'd been defrocked.

His resolute march along the flagstone floor was set to the resonance of his footsteps. The steel plates on the heels and toes of his black, leather shoes rang out piercing, rhythmic, double-clicks that softened as they echoed against the old walls. It sounded like he was bellringing.

The old man looked like a titan.

I followed him, looking up and at his back, as though I was a child following in its father's hasty footsteps. I was struggling to keep up. He had my vestments folded over one arm.

He got to the door of the old vestry and barked at the sentries, *Open it!*

As he strode in the heavy, oak door closed behind him and I was left staring at it.

Part 1: Assembly

That morning a letter came. It was from him. After the usual niceties this is what he wrote.

> I've taken two liberties for which I make no apologies.
>
> The first is that I have decided not to acknowledge, formally, your resignation. I will be recording your current absence from priestly life as a sabbatical. That leaves things open-ended should you wish to reconsider your position in a year or so.
>
> Second, I have contacted the bishop of the diocese in which you currently reside. He's an old friend and I have asked him to keep an eye on you. I want to make sure that you are being cared for if I possibly can.
>
> It's my understanding that he's asked one of his archdeacons to contact you. I'm not sure he's the right man for you if I'm being candid, so I'm writing both to let you know and to warn you: the archdeacon is a cleric with an MBA and something of a speciality in what's called Human Resources these days.
>
> I struggle to think of myself as a resource in any sense of that word but, management-speak notwithstanding, I hope he will represent our best intentions to you well enough.
>
> I'd like to think you have not written off your vocation entirely. It is clear to me, and others, that you have the makings of a fine priest.
>
> With my best wishes,
>
> +

Part 2: Purification

Then Jesus said to his disciples, "Truly I tell you, it will be hard for a rich person to enter the kingdom of heaven. Again, I tell you, it is easier for a camel to go through the eye of a needle than for someone who is rich to enter the kingdom of God."

Matthew 19:23-24

- 24 -

There's a beautiful story in the Gospels about a blind man.

Blind Bartimaeus has heard that Jesus the healer is in town and he's set his heart on recovering his sight.

Jesus! he calls at the top of his desperate voice, *Jesus! Have mercy on me!*

I love the text's account of those around him trying to silence him. In England, we would hush him because that kind of display is embarrassing. It's just not the done thing. How have we managed to turn timidity into a virtue?

But brave Bartimaeus pays no attention to his critics and shouts even louder. He's a blind man on a mission. I've always pictured him as a cantankerous New-Yorker.

Jesus hears his cry, and commands, *Call him here!*

And then the text gets to the heart of the matter, but it's smuggled in before the climax.

When the blind man hears that he has been granted an audience with Jesus, we are told that he throws off his cloak.

It's downhill from there: he springs to his feet and comes to Jesus, who asks, *What do you want me to do for you?* Bartimaeus is uncompromising: *My teacher, let me see again.* Jesus is equally uncompromising: *Go! Your faith has made you well.*

What the text should tell us, but doesn't, is that once Bartimaeus had thrown off his cloak he never put it on again. He spent the rest of his life as naked as an earthworm.

Stark-bollock-naked.

Unless we are stripped of our ways of seeing, our assumptions, convictions, and agendas, we are in the dark. Actually, it's worse than that. The Jesus of John's Gospel puts his finger on it when he says to the Pharisees: *If you were blind, you would not have sin. But now that you say, "We see," your sin remains.*

- 25 -

So, what do you make of it all? I asked.

Well, it's all about nudity and not a lot else.

Nudity?

Yes, he nodded.

My silence seemed to unnerve me far more than him and I hated these periods where I searched for something to say in return.

What do you mean?

It begins with the nudity of the garden and ends with the nudity of the cross, he added.

He felt no need to explain himself further.

From somewhere in my mind a text from Mark's Gospel surfaced and I found myself thinking about the Naked Fugitive. It's a mysterious detail that's only to be found in Mark's account of the events in the Garden of Gethsemane.

Jesus has taken his close followers to the Garden and asked them to keep watch while he prays. He wrestles with a profound distress and grief, finally surrendering to his impending death with the words he taught us in the Our Father: Not my will but yours be done.

The disciples, as is often the case in Mark's account, make a very poor showing of themselves by repeatedly falling asleep on their Rabbi.

The lynch mob arrives, led by Judas, whose lips seal the betrayal with a kiss, and he is arrested and handed over to those who will end up killing him. He describes this moment as 'his hour' and proclaims that the scripture must be fulfilled while every one of the disciples deserted him and fled.

And then, as if out of nowhere and standing alone, we read the following words: "A certain young man was following him, wearing nothing but a linen cloth. They caught hold of him, but he left the linen cloth and ran off naked."

Maybe a portal opened for that young fugitive in that Garden on that day? And maybe the key to that portal lay under the linen cloth he was wearing?

Maybe that Naked Fugitive was the first fruit of Jesus' Passion?

If you don't know this, what is it that you think you were offering as a priest? His words punctured the play of my thoughts.

I'm not really sure, I stammered. *I think that's why I am here: to find out.*

Well, I can only make you one promise.

What's that? I asked.

That from those who have nothing, even what they have will be taken away.

- 26 -

It was early winter.

People are so ready to take offence, I said. *It's a very contemporary addiction.*

A crisp frost had given way to bright sunshine.

He laughed at this and asked, *Who have you offended?*

Not me, I explained. *The vicar, on Sunday.*

We were browsing among the stalls in the farmer's market. It was a busy Saturday morning.

You're going to church? he asked.

From time to time, I replied. *Yes.*

He looked bemused.

Anyway, she preached on Jesus calling the Canaanite woman a dog.

Ah, he said. *OK. What did she make of it?*

I was watching Philo as we picked our way through the market. He needed restraining, especially near the fresh meat stalls.

I'm not altogether sure, I said. *I think it troubled her.*

The woman at the pet food stall saw us coming and beamed. She loved the dog, and he knew it.

It's a tough one, I continued. *She's desperate to find evidence that Jesus was somehow sensitive to the feminist thing. In this story, he really isn't. Neither is he polite, which is another deeply cherished dream of hers.*

I could see him laughing at this out of the corner of my eye. I was busy trying to keep Philo from the produce.

It's as though she's lit a fire of hope for his sensitivity to women and his decency and this story threatens to put it out, I continued.

Maybe she doesn't yet know that all our cherished illusions are destined to drown, he said.

It sounded like a portent, addressed more to me than to the vicar I was talking about.

Maybe, I said, without knowing that for myself with any certainty at all.

We walked on and headed up the high street.

It's harder when you discover that the abyss in which the drowning happens is Jesus himself, he said. *I feel for her.*

When did you suddenly become so sentimental? I asked. *I was just irritated by all the earnest, self-righteous squirming.*

Oh, he said, *I don't really care about the self-righteousness or the squirming. And there will come a day when you don't either.*

We turned into Abbey Road.

She obviously doesn't yet know what a compliment it is to be called a dog, he said after a few paces.

We walked on and towards the abbey. It could look ominous, but today, with its sandstone bathed in the sunshine, it seemed to glow with an inviting warmth.

I love being a dog, he said.

- 27 -

We met when, finally, I was exhausted. I just hadn't admitted it to myself yet. It threatened to look too much like a good, old-fashioned, nervous breakdown.

You might call it providence, but I couldn't because that makes a claim to some kind of knowing and I couldn't say that I knew anything at all. Discernment is the name some people give to it, while they've still got the energy to pretend that they can see the hand of God at work in their lives.

I'd almost stopped pretending.

I spent as much time as I could in his company. Sometimes I saw him every day and sometimes days would go by before I, inevitably, knocked on his door once again.

I had nowhere else to go.

Why did you call yourself a dog the other day? I asked.

It seemed pretty literal to me. He didn't say he was like a dog.

Because it's true, he said.

He was cooking. His kitchen was filled with the smell of onions, garlic, and thyme.

He stirred the pan with a long, wooden spoon and said, "*I fled Him, down the nights and down the days.*"

Then, he looked at me and barked. I still don't know how he kept a straight face.

Philo wandered in from the fireplace in the lounge and stood to attention in front of him.

You mean, the poem? I asked. *The Hound of Heaven?*[12]

That's the one, he said, with a broad smile.

I knew bits of the poem, and after a while I recited,

> "I fled Him, down the arches of the years;
> I fled Him, down the labyrinthine ways
> Of my own mind; and in the mist of tears
> I hid from Him…"

He listened as I chanted the verses, rhythmically.

Wonderful, isn't it? he asked.

I'm not sure, I said.

It is when you've stopped running and hiding, he said.

He held my eyes with a reassuring look and continued,

> "But with unhurrying chase,
> And unperturbèd pace,
> Deliberate speed, majestic instancy,

They beat—and a Voice beat
More instant than the Feet—
'All things betray thee, who betrayest Me.'"

He moved away from the stove and sat, opposite me, at his kitchen table. The silence made me very uneasy.

After what seemed like a long time, he spoke.

Why do you think you ended up here?

Initially, I wasn't sure, I replied.

And now?

I hesitated before saying, *For spiritual direction?*

His laugher erupted at this point. Even the disconcerted look on my face couldn't stop him and my anger flared up.

You can be a cruel bastard!

That's not the right way to put it, he said, still laughing.

Spiritual direction! he mocked, as he shook his head. *Doesn't that sound grand?*

I'm going home, I said, as I stood and called to Philo, who looked up from his spot by the fire without moving.

The dog knows what I am, and he thinks you should stay, he said.

I turned to him, and before I could say anything, he continued, *I can't be a cruel bastard.*

What the fuck does that mean? I shouted. My temper was still running hot.

I'm an undertaker, not a spiritual director, he said. *I only work with the dead.*

He held my angry gaze calmly, without any expression or gesture of appeasement. It was as though he was saying the most obvious thing in the world.

When you realise that, you won't call it cruelty anymore, he said.

I left Philo with him that day. Maybe it was an excuse to go back.

- 28 -

When I did go back the next day, he didn't mention my storming out on him. The dog came gently up to me and rested his head against my leg.

I've come for Philo, I said.

Right, he answered.

As I slipped on the dog's collar and lead, I hoped he would suggest I stayed, but he didn't.

His fire was roaring, and the place smelled of coffee. The winter, morning sun was streaming through the windows.

How was he? I asked.

Happy enough, he said. *He slept by the fire.*

Philo sat quietly at my feet as I stood looking out of his window at the cold, hard ground outside.

Are you going? he asked.

I didn't respond.

You know, he said, *God always seems like an enemy when we are devoted to our own project.*

I don't have any bloody projects! I shot back.

He didn't reply immediately. We stood, looking at each other for a while.

When he did speak it was with a profound compassion that I had not seen in him before.

You are your own project, he said.

I didn't answer.

That's why you take such offence when it's being dismantled.

There was something in what he said that struck a deep chord. It was a chord I recognised but didn't really understand.

He came up to me then and put his hands on my shoulders.

You know, there's nothing in the world like quitting that project, he said.

I was staring at the floor, trying to conceal the shame and rising sense of grief that took hold of me as he spoke.

Have some coffee, he said. *It's good.*

All I could do was nod.

- 29 -

I ended up staying all day. We drank coffee, cooked, talked, and walked Philo.

Later in the afternoon, as dusk began to settle in, he said, *Are you sure you want to do this?*

I think so, I replied.

You've got to understand something first, though, he said.

What's that?

If you stay around it will end up costing you everything, he answered.

There was no particular emotion in his voice. It was as though he was reciting a simple fact.

Time to decide whether you can actually build the tower or wage the war.

It was a reference to Luke's Gospel and a passage that depicts the same choice that I was being presented with: "For which of you, intending to build a tower, does not first sit down and estimate the cost, to see whether he has enough to complete it? Otherwise, when he has laid a foundation and is not able to finish, all who see it will begin to ridicule him, saying, 'This fellow began to build and was not able to finish.' Or what king, going out to wage war against another king, will not sit down first and consider whether he is able with ten thousand to oppose the one who comes against him with twenty thousand? If he cannot, then, while the other is still far away, he sends a delegation and asks for the terms of peace."

And you can go any time you like, he continued. *All you have to do is let me know you are asking for the terms of peace.*

I sat and thought for a while. I suppose I was somewhat reassured by my option to leave if things got too weird.

I've got one major reservation you need to know about, he said.

What's that? I asked.

Your vocation, he said.

Oh? Is that an issue?

Yes, he replied. *The people I usually see can't survive in church, let alone work for one.*

We sat in silence and I noticed a feeling of sadness and loss begin to creep over me. It was time to go.

He stood up and called Philo to him. The dog sat in front of him quietly while the collar was slipped around his neck.

You can tell me your reservations another day, he said, as he handed me the lead.

I don't think I've got any, I said.

He chuckled quietly in response, as he saw me to the door.

We'll find them, he said.

- 30 -

I've read that in Zen they sometimes compare the face-to-face interviews between a student and the teacher to being in a cave with a tiger. The tiger's job in the cave is twofold: to block the exit, and to tear the silky, suffocating veil of ignorance to shreds.

It's nothing other than a work of love but the gentle Jesus is nowhere to be found.

Truth be told, I never found the Lion of Judah that gentle. My pharisaic ego always suspected he'd tear the robes off me if he ever got a hold of me.

Why does it trouble you so much that you have nothing to give? he asked, one afternoon. *It's far better than thinking you do.*

How do you mean? I asked.

As usual I was finding him difficult to follow.

People don't want the kind of love you've been wanting to give. They'd rather have the truth, he said.

I still don't follow you, I stammered.

When you stop acting like you've got something to give then you can just keep them company.

He turned and got up at this point and headed for his bathroom.

That's what they really want, he said, as he walked down his hall.

When he got back to the living room I was sitting on his sofa, staring out of the window.

He continued to talk about love.

He who humbles himself wishes to be exalted, he said. *The Reverend Father Nietzsche knew it better than you do.* [13]

I thought of Sunday's sermon on sacrificial giving and remembered for a moment how it exhausted me. I had heard that song, in one arrangement or another, so many times.

Why is it that Christians often preach on the necessity of loving one another without acknowledging just how impossible that is?

I've never managed it.

When you love, you're on manoeuvres, nothing else.

He was on a roll.

You need the poor more than the poor need you.

So how do I stop doing that? I asked.

You can't, he replied abruptly.

That's not very helpful at all, I mumbled.

He sat quietly for a while before adding, *Not until you realise that when you look at them you are looking in a mirror.*

Then he looked me square in the eyes for a moment and smiled.

Don't you see? he asked, *There are no givers and takers; no right and left hands.*

It reminded me of Jesus' words in the Gospel of Matthew: "When you give, do not let your left hand know what your right hand is doing."

Part 2: Purification

John Steinbeck once wrote that giving is the most overrated virtue of all the shoddy virtues, I said quietly.

Actually, he went further than that: giving builds up the ego of the giver, makes him superior and higher and larger than the receiver. Dressing oneself up as a giver brings the same sense of superiority as getting does. Philanthropy is often just another kind of spiritual avarice.[14]

I should have anticipated his reply before it came along to interrupt the train of my thoughts.

You've come here to give me a taste of your knowledge about Steinbeck? Is that for my benefit, or yours?

Ouch! I said, with a smile on my face. *I'll keep the wine I brought to myself then, shall I? Would that be for my benefit or yours?*

He laughed.

Steinbeck wasn't talking about wine, he said. *He may have been talking about Church, though.*

I had no reply to that.

Now, where is that bottle? he asked, as he headed for his kitchen to get a corkscrew.

- 31 -

The pub was slowly filling up with people.

Men who had skipped off work early came first, mostly in pairs, and occupied the stools that ran along the front of the long bar. The quiet had amplified into a murmur.

Why did you seem surprised that I go to church from time to time? I asked.

He was scanning faces as they came in, looking for people he recognised.

Do you ever go? I continued.

No! he said, before laughing. *I couldn't stand it any longer.*

The Emperor's New Clothes, he continued. *The whole thing seemed to me to be a colossal exercise in self-deception.*

The pub was buzzing with the happy murmur of end-of-day conversations and an open fire roared in the corner.

We were talking mission with nothing to offer.

He drained his pint glass and asked if I wanted another, before adding, *Do you know how ridiculous it is to be proclaiming a salvation you don't really possess?*

Yes, I think I do, I replied.

I had been doing it for years.

While he was at the bar, I looked around the room and remembered that I had always planned to retire to a pub.

Did you point all this out to them? I asked when he got back to the table.

No, he said, as he sat down. *I've already told you that I was a coward and lacked eloquence.*

He paused, before saying, without any hint of regret, *But I did tell the priest he was an arsehole.*

I'm not surprised he didn't like that, I said.

It was true, he said. *He was preaching revival and wouldn't see that by doing that he was declaring his own bankruptcy.*

I'm not sure I follow you, I said.

People who have God don't constantly preach about his coming, he replied. *If he had admitted to his own poverty I would've stayed.*

We drank in silence for a while.

A good pub always feels like home to me, I said.

The smell of ale and the smoke was soul-warming.

I always knew you were an orphan, he said with a smile.

- 32 -

Later, as we walked away from the pub, he could see I was preoccupied.

Are you busy straining out gnats and swallowing camels? he asked.

What?

You're bothered that I called the priest an arsehole, he said.

We walked on in silence for a while.

I think it was a bit uncalled for, I replied.

Why? he asked. *You're a priest and you can be an arsehole, can't you?*

An evening rain had wet the pavement and it glistened under the streetlamps.

Maybe you'd be happier if I had called him a fool? he asked.

We turned a corner and headed for the alleyway that led to the edge of town.

Or a charlatan?

Part 2: Purification

The alleyway was narrow. I walked ahead of him and he called over my shoulder, *Why is it that my calling him an arsehole troubles you more than the possibility he might be a fraud?*

He may have been a fool because he didn't know he was a fraud, I said.

I didn't know whether, by defending this particular priest, I was making excuses for myself and my own ministry.

He was a priest! he mocked. *It was his job to know whether or not he was a fraud, not mine!*

We got to the end of the alley and stood for a moment, side by side, looking up at the dark, looming hill that led up towards the woods and the paddocks beyond.

His place was a good thirty-minute walk.

You're like the church you serve, he said. *You're busy covering Jesus' nudity as though his dick was the real obscenity of the cross.*

I turned away after that, leaving him to trek to his cottage alone.

Philo and I headed home.

- 33 -

You're rude, I said.

Actually, it's worse than that. You can be really offensive.

He was nodding but all he said, with an infuriating, smug smile, was, *Here comes the first reservation.*

Well? I asked.

You want me to explain myself? he replied.

I hadn't seen him for three days.

We were on our way to the greengrocer's. It was cold and grey. The dark sky hung low and a fine drizzle covered us as we walked.

I tell you what, he said. *I'll explain myself to you, and even dance to your tune, if you do something for me.*

OK, I replied. *What is it?*

Explain to me how you plan to heal yourself? he challenged.

I had no answer.

As he wiped his feet on the mat outside the greengrocer's door he muttered, *I thought the conversation about my egotism would come first.*

What? I said, unsure if I had heard him correctly.

He took a basket from the pile, headed for the root vegetables, and said, over his shoulder as he stepped into the shop, *Don't worry, it'll come up soon enough.*

I waited outside, with the dog.

- 34 -

Coming home was hard, I said.

Hard? he asked.

Yes. I knew it was the right thing to do but there was also a feeling that I was coming home to a reckoning.

And did that happen? he enquired.

No. It didn't, I answered. *That's what's happening now.*

He laughed.

I didn't know then that I could find lots of ways of running away right here.

So, what happened? he pressed.

I got job after job, I answered.

And they helped?

No. Not at all.

I cast my mind back to some of them.

I watched friends making shedloads of money and tried to buy that dream too.

But you saw through it? he asked.

Hardly, I replied. *I just wasn't very good at making money.*

He smiled at that.

So, I couldn't tell you that money doesn't buy happiness because I've never really made any.

He nodded and said, *Yes, it's a catchphrase for the successful, I suppose.*

Or the envious, I added.

There's another option, of course. Camus apparently wrote that it's a spiritual kind of snobbery that makes people think they can be happy without money.[15]

It was still early in December, but the first frost had come very late that year, so he decided we would pick blackthorn berries to make sloe-gin. The low-hanging, afternoon sun shone in the crisp, winter air.

Then, one day, I had this strange experience, I picked up my story again. *I was trying to sell a bloke a franchise and I suddenly saw something.*

What? he asked, turning to me.

I saw that he was a Christian, I answered. *Don't ask me how but I saw it. It was as though scales fell from my eyes and I saw his soul.*

He went back to his picking.

So, I just asked him, I said. *Outright. It must have been weird for him.*

Why? he asked.

Because I didn't even acknowledge that it was a bizarre question, I answered. *Normally I apologise before I say something risky, just to cover myself and give myself an exit strategy.*

Our bags were getting full, but we pressed on.

I'm going to make twelve bottles this year, he said.

We picked in silence for a while. Philo was meandering in the woodland beyond the blackthorn shrubs.

How did he respond? he asked, eventually.

He just said, yes, I said. *That's all. Just, yes.*

And you ended up in his church? he asked.

I nodded. *But it took a few months to build up the courage,* I said.

I remembered putting it off, week after week.

But yes. I ended up in his Church one Sunday morning in mid-winter.

What was that like? he asked.

It was happy-clappy, I answered.

Anyone who is familiar with the endless round of preaching, teaching, worship, prayer meetings, house-groups, and spiritual warfare knows that there isn't much more to say than that.

How on earth I ended up spending seven years in a church with not much more to say than that remains a mystery to me.

It's all a desperate ploy. An attempt to trigger revival, which is the real god of the piece.

Actually, that is open for more refinement: the revival pictured always involves the elect being filled with unprecedented levels of power, so the real god of the piece is the elect themselves, transformed by a visitation of the Holy Spirit, into superheroes.

It's a narcissistic, seductive dream.

Then, one day, towards the end of my time there, a book was sent to me by mistake, I continued.

Mistake? he asked.

Yes. I'd ordered a book, I don't remember what, and when I opened the parcel, I was looking at the front cover of Shirley du Boulay's biography of St Teresa of Avila.[16]

And you read it? he pressed.

Yes. In secret.

The church I was in considered all things Catholic and mystical to be squarely in the realm of the occult. But I was ripe for going off the rails by that stage. Something inside was just not believing it anymore. I was beginning to go off-message.

He laughed. *Good for you.*

And how did you find it? Teresa of Avila's story?

Well, it was like fine dining, I answered.

Like realising I'd been eating the same evangelical crap, served up in forty different colours for years, and I'd suddenly tripped up and landed in the best restaurant I could imagine.

So, you devoured it? he asked.

I did. And a lot more, I nodded. *I started sneaking back to Mass from time to time during the week and even bought myself a rosary.*

He chuckled to himself.

I was remembering those thrilling days. I re-immersed myself in the culture of the church I had been born into and raised in. I had never paid much attention to it as a child. It didn't take long before I ended up seeking re-admission.

So, your Catholic episode began? he asked.

Yes, I affirmed.

Jesus, Mary, and Joseph! he winked.

He was watching me carefully.

From the frying pan and into the fire. From the inerrancy of the bible to the infallibility of the Pope.

He was on a roll.

You went from scriptural fundamentalism to sacramental fundamentalism. And all because you couldn't resist the sweet song of the mystics.

He was right. I still can't resist that sweet song.

And how long before you realised that the fine dining of Catholicism would turn to ash in your mouth as surely as the evangelical food did?

I'm not sure, I said.

You will be, he answered.

I couldn't accept certain things.

Top of the list was the corrupting inevitability of clericalism. Not just the sexual degenerates, and there were plenty of those, just ask anyone who's been to an English Catholic boarding school as I had.

It was the whole culture of clericalism itself. The Catholic clergy is an elitist caste, as powerful as any.

There's a saying of Jesus about good trees not producing bad fruit and I think it can be applied to theological doctrines. There's a case for saying that the theology of priesthood has produced a pretty toxic harvest.

Intimately linked to the doctrine of priesthood is the doctrine of the sacraments, through which the church has made herself the administrator of salvation.

Grace is what we all are, he interrupted. *It's our very being, we who are created in the image of God. How on earth they have managed to convince people that they are the exclusive dispensers of grace and being is beyond me.*

He was laughing and shaking his head. *They have franchised the air we all breathe.*

I heard his words and understood them, but I was still a long way from knowing they were true.

Anyway, I said. *It all made me too angry, so I left.*

And all the while you were hankering after priesthood yourself? He wasn't going to let me off the hook.

Maybe we could put it down to envy? he suggested.

I didn't answer.

You had a bad case of what gripped Joseph's brothers, he continued.

What do you mean by that?

Well, they wanted his coat of many colours and you wanted the costumes of the priests.

I had never put my hostility down to envy. What's more, I had never put myself forward for the Catholic priesthood.

But something in me winced at his words.

No matter now, he said. *Hopefully, you can see now that it's not a costume worth having.*

I'm still not sure.

- 35 -

Do you believe in prophecies? I asked.

Whose? he answered. *Which ones?*

There are so many, he added.

I smiled. They were fair questions. *I'll take that as a no, then. Shall I?*

He laughed.

I think most people who identify as prophets are full of shit, he said.

Most of the ones I knew of had been prophesying revivals, of one sort or another, for years, and getting it wrong, in one way or another, for years. It did all seem to be an unseemly blend of egotism and delusion.

There's one I believe, he said.

Which one? I asked.

He stopped, turned to me, and pointed right at my head, before quoting Jesus' words in Matthew's Gospel, with mock-Shakespearean gravitas: *Do you see this great building? Not one stone will be left here upon another; all will be thrown down.*

You say the same thing again and again, I said.

I do, he affirmed.

That's because there's only one prophecy, he continued.

And that is?

Death and resurrection, he said. *The fall and the rise. That's all.*

He turned away from me.

And at least I don't make any money from it. That ought to comfort you.

- 36 -

Later, we were sitting on a bench at the market square watching the traders pack their stalls up for the day. I was smoking, it was cold, and there was a sense in the air that Christmas was on its way. It makes the winter more bearable.

I like Sartre, he said, *because I made the same mistake as him.*

What mistake is that?

I confused things with their names: that is belief.[17]

After a moment or two, I asked him when it was that he realised he'd got it wrong.

When the curtain was torn in two, from top to bottom, the same thing happened to the names, he replied.

How do we know when we have spun words into worlds?

I'm not sure it's possible without a gadfly and it was beginning to dawn on me that Harvey had a method, of sorts. It became apparent when I would come out with some Christian vapidity or other, using it as though it was a reality in my experience rather than a speculation I had inherited from the tradition.

Socrates was famous for it. It's even called the Socratic method.[18] People who are good at it, and polite, might phrase it like this, often with a wry smile on their lips: "Let's unpack that a little, shall we?"

Harvey wasn't polite. He didn't care about himself enough to care about that.

We Christians are particularly susceptible to it with our creeds and our pithy bible verses and prayers, handed down by the saints. Not to mention the great theologians from whom whole schools of Christianity have evolved. In these schools, hosts of people speak a similar language and inhabit similar worlds.

With our insistence that somehow the Word became Flesh, we have repaid the favour by insisting that the Flesh has become Words. Any Christian service of worship betrays that fact.

I wish they'd all just bloody well stop talking! he said one day.

He had a point.

We have, somehow, fallen into a kind of fundamentalism. It's easy to spot when certain groups claim the inerrancy of the scripture: they fall into a crass bibliolatry that the rest of us can sneer at.

But we are all guilty of some kind of idolatry, aren't we? Our progressive ones may be more subtle, but they are every bit as fanciful. To go to a fancy-dress party disguised as Albert Einstein doesn't make the pretence any less a pretence than going as Fred Flintstone.

These glib Christian phrases may have originated in the minds of people who were intimately acquainted with the reality they point to, but to manipulate a Buddhist saying, most of us seem devoted to the fingers that point to the moon, rather than stripping our clothes off and embracing the moon to whom the fingers point.

She's very beautiful, the moon. Perhaps too beautiful to bear?

- 37 -

So, it was for freedom that Christ has set us free, you say?

I had been talking about St Paul.

He looked irritated. I had the impression that in his mind he was taking his coat off and rolling up his sleeves before asking me to step outside for a moment.

Yes, I replied, nervously.

You're free, then? he pressed.

In what sense? I asked.

He pushed on.

You need clarification?

Yes, I do, I said. *In what sense?*

Free to let the dead bury their own dead? It was a challenge. He looked fierce and defiant.

That verse is...

Stop! he growled, cutting me off with a ruthless tone.

I must have looked distressed and embarrassed for a second because he took a more conciliatory tone.

Just stop, he said, warmly, changing his tone. It was an invitation rather than a rebuke.

You've got nothing to give here.

- 38 -

My house was beginning to crumble. I could feel it.

I don't know whether it was his words acting like a battering ram on my Christian identity or the fact that I was simply outgrowing an outdated set of assumptions. Looking back, one thing is clear to me: I was ripe for undermining.

In January, after the distractions of the Christmas season, with nothing but two months of deep winter to look forward to, things took a turn for the worse. A heavy, sluggish gloom seemed to descend on me.

I was in mourning. I've never known anything like it.

When I told him, all he said was, *Good! About time.*

I must have looked confused because he continued, *Well, you're the one who told me you were ready to be sick for a while.*

He smiled at me.

I was wondering when you were going to get tired enough to mean what you said.

If anything, he besieged the walls of my house more ruthlessly after that.

- 39 -

People are addicted to stories, he said.

And that's a problem? I asked.

For you, now, yes. A big problem.

I sat, waiting for him to elaborate.

You have already cast yourself in so many stories, he said.

He had his back to me as he spoke. He was washing dishes.

You've played the rebel and the romantic; the addict and the lover; the husband and the father; the prophet and the priest.

He paused as if he was searching for words.

Part 2: Purification

And every time the story has changed you have called it progress, growth, or, worse still, transformation. Aren't you tired of your stories?

I'm exhausted, I nodded.

He turned and looked at me, handed me a tea towel and said, *You dry.*

I picked up a wet plate from the draining board while he continued.

The problem with stories is that you only ever get to appear as an actor, and that's a shadowy existence.

That reminds me of the Hebrew concept of Sheol, I said.[19]

He shot back quickly, *And now you come here to play the thoughtful academic?*

When I was with him, almost everything I said and thought seemed like a pose.

How do I stop? I asked.

You can't, he replied, without any hesitation at all. *If you could, you'd just turn that into another story.*

That would be unbearable, he chuckled.

You'd just play the enlightened sage!

I hate talking to you at times, I said.

95

Well of course you do, he nodded.

There's nothing in the plot for you here, except death.

- 40 -

At night, I tried to survive in the face of the darkness that began to haunt me, more and more.

The deep winter was brutal. I hated being home alone at Forge Lane.

It wasn't just the darkness in my mind, there was a living darkness at work on and in me. It nudged me, especially when I distracted myself and got lost in menial tasks around the house.

The dog's reassuring presence was my anchor.

I learnt something then. No one comes to God in company. It's a fearful thing but a true thing. At some point the threshold at the proverbial narrow gate must be crossed alone. I remember realising that one night when Harvey's profound solitude struck me.

Maybe that's what he taught me better than anything: how to be truly alone.

You've got to allow your loneliness to flower into solitude, he would say. *Don't fight your loneliness.*

I ran from it like it was terminal, and he could sense and see that.

Be lonely, he would say.

That's where your fathers and mothers and brothers and sisters are.

- 41 -

In spite of his advice, I headed to his place as often as I could.

When he wasn't in, Philo and I would weave our way back through the icy, silver woods and back down the hill to our own house. It seemed a pointless exercise but one that fitted my predicament perfectly. I was going around in circles, heading for a goal that didn't seem to be there when I thought I'd arrived.

He seemed intimately familiar with my mental state.

Can you describe how it happened to you in layman's terms?

He shook his head. *No. I don't think I can,* he said.

Have a go. Please.

After a moment where he was clearly groping for words he said, quietly, *I was ruthlessly stripped by a kind of fire.*

That sounds painful and frightening, I said. *Was it?*

He nodded.

Yes, it was, and worse than that, he said.

After a moment, a smile broke across his face and he continued, *Until, at the end of it, I found myself in his discarded robe.*

- 42 -

When I did see him, I clung to him and ransacked his mind for hints about my own condition. I was looking for a thread in his story that I could interweave with my own.

It's a perfect example of trying to ride on another's coattails.

If you want to know what it was really like, read Gerard Manley Hopkins, he said. *It's in his Terrible Sonnets.*

Do you have a copy? I asked.

No, he said. *I remember some of one of them, though.*

He recited bits of it, then, from memory, in a way that made me sense his deep familiarity with the words.

> "No worst, there is none. Pitched past pitch of grief,
> More pangs will, schooled at forepangs, wilder wring."

He looked at me, then. He looked sombre. Even stern. There was no pity in it at all. It was a warning.

It gets worse, you see? he said. *These are only the forepangs.*

He picked up his recitation again.

> "Comforter, where, where is your comforting?
> Mary, mother of us, where is your relief?
> My cries heave, herds-long; huddle in a main, a chief
> Woe, world-sorrow; on an age-old anvil wince and sing…"[20]

There was something in the poem I could identify. A desperation. I winced as the words found a pocket of recognition somewhere deep inside my own distress. It's a difficult thing to watch a man tormented, but it's even harder to listen to his despair because none of us wants to visit that cave in ourselves.

World sorrow, I repeated. *That's a good way to put it.*

Yes, he nodded.

And it's an age-old anvil, he said. *It might disappoint you to know you're not the only one.*

He was wrong. I was relieved.

- 43 -

By our next meeting I had bought a copy of the Terrible Sonnets.

One thing troubled me: it was far from clear that Hopkins was a mystic. He wasn't officially recognised as such by the Catholic church to which he belonged and there were plenty of people ready to diagnose him with a chronic manic-depressive illness, not that anyone has ever worked out exactly what that is.

I'm always suspicious of these retroactive diagnoses, and the theological world is full of them. They are normally written by people who have never had a religious experience, and there's no point in telling them that the only way to know such things is to go through such things for oneself and see what comes out of the other side.

It might be called walking through the valley of the shadow of death.

The danger is that there might not be another side to the valley. It might be a no-through road.

That was the fear I was struggling with.

I read to him.

> "O the mind, mind has mountains; cliffs of fall
> Frightful, sheer, no-man-fathomed. Hold them cheap
> May who ne'er hung there."

He was nodding.

> "Nor does long our small
> Durance deal with that steep or deep. Here! creep,
> Wretch, under a comfort serves in a whirlwind: all
> Life death does end and each day dies with sleep."

When I had finished, he sat in silence for a good few minutes.

When he spoke, he said, *I thought Hopkins may have been mad until I hung there too.*

- 44 -

My mind toyed with images of him alone and I wondered how he coped. It was easier than facing my own desperation and feeling of isolation.

So, the next time I visited, I asked him.

I didn't cope, he said, in a very matter-of-fact tone. *No one copes with it; it kills you.*

Oh?

That's the point, he continued.

It kills you and that's when you discover that the no-man-fathomed cliffs and the frightful steep and deep are Christ-fathomed.

He looked at me then and said, *He is the only one that survives them.*

They are his home, and they became mine when I found myself in him.

- 45 -

It's deep waters, I said. *It's like deep, cold, black waters.*

I was remembering a Psalm. I had prayed them often enough.

> Save me, O God,
>   for the waters have come up to my neck.
> I sink in deep mire,
>   where there is no foothold;
> I have come into deep waters,
>   and the flood sweeps over me.

How did you cope with this darkness? I asked him again.

In different ways, he said.

We were at his place and I was lying on his sofa. He was almost flat on his back on the reclining armchair, staring at his ceiling.

There's no way of avoiding the pain, you know.

I can't remember which one it was, but a cello suite played softly in the background.

But it does help to have someone who gets it to talk to.

Did you have that? I asked. *Someone to talk to about all this?*

No, he said, *not really.*

But you were in a monastery? I protested. I was confused.

Oh, don't be so naive! he snapped.

The cello was intoning its melancholic rhythms and we listened for a while.

So, I asked again, *you didn't say. How did you cope with this darkness and pain?*

I drank for a while, he answered, without taking his eyes off the ceiling.

It's as good a remedy as any, you know.

You drank for a while? I asked.

I hadn't expected that answer at all.

How was that a remedy? Didn't it make things worse?

Maybe for some people, he said. *For me it just delayed the inevitable.*

I don't follow, I said.

I was struggling to understand and cope with the place I found myself in.

I couldn't be sure that I wasn't going through some sort of psychological episode and I was frantically trying to get my bearings in a land without coordinates or any recognisable landmarks.

There are all kinds of ways of avoiding the darkness, when it closes in on you, he said. *It's very frightening and disorientating to begin with, so some redouble their efforts at prayer and all things spiritual.*

And that's a strategy of avoidance? I asked.

Yes. Nothing else. He continued, *And what's more, it's dangerous, especially when there's someone who doesn't know what they are doing advising the person.*

I was curious. In my own desperation I suppose I was looking for some clue as to how I was going to survive.

What are the others? I asked.

There are lots, he said. *Some get enamoured with the aestheticism of the thing and lose themselves in that. Others in relationships. Others quit and run. I slept a lot, too.*

And the drinking? I pressed.

It just numbed the pain, softened the anger, blunted the fear, and eased the loneliness for a while, that's all, he said. *Drinking blurs the edges.*

We sat in silence for a while.

Just being in his company was a comfort to me on that occasion. I took solace from the idea that someone had passed this way before and relief from the possibility that I wasn't going mad. At least that's what I hoped.

Part 2: Purification

When did it stop? I asked, after a while.

When did what stop? he asked.

The drinking, I answered.

Oh, right, he said. *When I eventually understood that the darkness was God and that it was my friend.*

This darkness is my friend? I asked.

Yes, he said.

But it needs to do its work on you for a while before you get to see that. Until then, you will think it's an enemy and there will be plenty of people ready to confirm that.

He started laughing, quietly at this point. I watched him and realised he was reliving a memory.

You never know, he said, *some kind folks might even work very hard to intercede for you. You might even have the exorcists hovering to deliver you from God.*

He was chuckling to himself and shaking his head.

- 46 -

I woke on his sofa.

He had lit the fire, which now burned steadily in the grate, and I was covered with one of his grey blankets. Philo was curled up in his usual spot. I glanced at my watch. It was just gone four in the morning.

Morning, he called.

The voice came from his kitchen.

Morning, I answered.

I wasn't sure how long I'd been asleep. All I remember is the tail end of a conversation on darkness and then I must have drifted off.

Sorry. I fell asleep on you.

Don't worry about it, he said.

It was still black outside, but the room was lit with a glow from the fireplace.

Tea? he asked.

Please, I answered.

We sat and drank and then he made toast.

There was nothing much to talk about. I had never felt this at ease, at least not as far back as I can vividly remember. We took turns making a fuss of Philo, who meandered back and forth between us, looking for affection. He kept the fire burning. There was nowhere to go and nothing at all to do.

A few hours later, just before dawn, he said, *This darkness, it's love, you know.*

Maybe, I said. *But I am scared.*

He nodded.

It's a fire, too, he said. *It feels cold and alien now, but, in time, it'll fill and warm your world and make itself your home.*

I hope so, I said.

- 47 -

The thought of leaving the safety of his place and returning to mine, filled me with dread.

Why did you say that praying is a waste of time at the moment? I asked.

Because it'll be an attempt to beat a retreat, he said. *Does that make sense to you?*

Yes, I said, *It kind of does. I don't know why or how, but it kind of does.*

As the day dawned, he said, *I'm off to bed for a couple of hours. I need to sleep.*

He put another couple of logs on the fire and told me to feel free to stay if I wanted to.

Thanks, I said, *I think I will.*

There's only one thing for you at this stage, he said.

What?

To let yourself burn, he answered.

As he turned and headed for his bed he said, *Might see you later.*

- 48 -

I was back at home and my mind kept wandering back to our conversations on prayer. I found it hard to believe that prayer was utterly useless, but I was sure that is what he said. So, the next time I saw him I brought it up again.

We were sitting in the café at Folio, the second-hand bookshop.

I need to ask you more about prayer, I said.

Wasn't I clear enough? he asked.

I'm not sure, I said. *That's the point.*

He picked up a copy of The Ladder of Divine Ascent by John Climacus that I had laid on the table.[21] I had browsed the religion section before he arrived, and I planned on buying it.

That won't do you much good at the moment, he said.

Just curious, I replied. *That's all.*

After a moment's silence he addressed my question again.

OK, he said. *Let's think this through. How do you talk to God at the moment?*

Well, I said, *when I decide to, I can't. I'm utterly at a loss. I don't have the words or the sense at all.*

That's good, he said. *And at other times?*

I stopped to think for a moment, then said, *When I feel the darkness pressing in, then I can talk.*

And what do you say? he asked.

Whatever comes up and out, I said. *It feels like this darkness is prizing open all the chambers of my heart and mind and their contents come bubbling up.*

What are those contents? he asked.

He was looking at me as I spoke.

Well, I say stuff like, 'Where are you, God?' a lot. And 'I'm lost?' And 'I'm terrified?'

He was nodding.

And *'I'm hurting.'* And *'I'm so angry.'*

So, if you want to call that prayer, that's fine, he said. *I was talking more about planned prayer, and methods and all that. Don't worry about what you're doing.*

We were quiet for a while, then. We sipped tea and looked around.

I haven't been here for a while, he said.

I love the smell, I said. *It comforts me.*

So many words, he sighed.

He was scanning the wall-to-wall bookshelves. They were packed to the rafters and there were books in piles on windowsills and sections of the floor.

So, if you want a rationale, you could say that your prayer life at the moment is one long confession, he said.

Confession?

Yes, he nodded. *The emptying of your mind and heart to God. Opening everything and presenting it, unvarnished, without explanation or justification.*

OK, that makes sense, I said.

It needs to go further now, he said.

How do you mean?

Well, he said, *if you're lost and angry and hurt and terrified and all those things, it's pretty difficult to imagine that you love God, even though your faith makes a very big deal of that.*

Something in me bristled as he spoke. The Greatest Commandment was so deeply lodged in my psyche, and from such a young age, that it had never crossed my mind that I could confess an antipathy to God.[22]

Under your confessions lie deeper truths that you need to confront.

I don't understand, I said.

Yes, you do, he replied nonchalantly. *All your anxieties are fuelled by some pretty basic assumptions.*

Like what? I asked.

Like, God is not good, he said. *Like, God doesn't love me. Even, God can't love me.*

He was keeping an eye on me as he spoke.

God is bad? Or, maybe even worse than that: God's not there?

It was as though he was speaking my mind for me. As I listened, the truth of his words struck me deeply. I was filled with fear, but that was quickly followed by an enormous feeling of relief.

Yes, I nodded. *It's true. That's how I feel.*

He got up and said, *You can pay. I'm off home.*

I didn't answer.

Go back to your house and tell God what you just told me, he said.

As he walked out, he turned and said, *Oh, and don't read Climacus.*

Put it back on the shelf.

- 49 -

There were days when, to be blunt, I couldn't function.

The curtains would stay drawn and I would quietly wander around in my own house. I'd make tea, smoke, pace, sit down, lie down, take a bath, talk to Philo.

Sitting still was difficult and painful. It felt like there was a fire lit inside me: I couldn't put it out; neither could I fan it into flame, so I could disappear into a pile of ash and stop being such a problem to myself.

I often slept so that I could avoid myself.

Looking back, I wish I'd had more courage. It all would have taken less time.

God, I'd say, you seem to love doing things in forties. I've been here for more than forty days and forty nights.

Noah's rains; Moses' mountain-top vigil; Goliath's taunting.

God. Goliath's taunting. Can't you muzzle him?

Elijah's walk; Ezekiel's lie-in; Jonah's preaching.

I would read the Pit Psalms and it worried me that they started to feel like home.

I wondered whether I would ever get to pray Psalm 139 and whisper, *If I make my bed in Sheol, behold, You are there.*

Maybe you're hidden in a deeper hell, I'd say.

How can you survive there?

- 50 -

Seeing him often didn't feel like it was helping, but I was driven by a compulsion that I didn't understand. He was the only person I could talk to.

I'm so fucked up, I said. *I'm the angriest man I know.*

He didn't reply.

And the trouble is, I can't shift it.

It had been a very difficult few days; days when all I seemed to be doing was exploring the darker recesses of my own mind. All I could find was anger, hatred, fear, and despair.

Weeping and gnashing of teeth, I said.

He nodded, as though the experience was not unfamiliar to him.

It was a windy, icy evening and we had just left the pub. The beer and the company had lightened my mood and I was grasping for words to describe what had been going on.

It's as though I'm on a tour of my own heart, I said. *Like I am being shown around my own temple.*

That's important, he said.

By this stage we were in the queue at the fish and chip shop and I waited in silence as he ordered, and then paid for two large portions of chips.

When they came, he asked, *Salt and vinegar?*

No vinegar, I answered.

We sat on the wall that ran alongside the abbey and ate. The chips warmed my hands in their newspaper wrapping.

There's nothing like hot chips on a belly full of beer, he said.

It was a curious experience. He didn't address or engage me in conversation about what I was saying but I had, nevertheless, a profound sense that he was accompanying me.

It hurts, I said.

He nodded but didn't look at me.

And it's very frightening. What if I'm this screwed up and this angry forever? What if I'm stuck?

He finished his chips and screwed up the newspaper.

You're not, he said, quite simply.

I stood to follow after him as he began to walk away, and he stopped me.

You need to go home, he said.

I can't face being alone, I replied.

You can, he responded with a quiet, reassuring tone.

You know, he said, *there was a saying in the monastery: your cell will teach you everything.*

I wasn't in the mood for spiritual-speak at all.

You don't say much all night and then when you speak it's to feed me a cliché!

Some clichés are true, he said, with a shrug.

You left the monastery and now you want to offer me the wisdom you rejected yourself? I protested.

He turned to face me and looked me straight in the eyes. There was nothing defiant in it at all. It was as though he was holding me up as he spoke.

I didn't reject all the monastic wisdom, he said. *I just told you I found a door and walked, that's all.*

That makes no sense at all, I replied.

It makes perfect sense, he said. *The door I found was in my cell.*

He paused.

Now, go home.

- 51 -

One of the great temptations in the spiritual wilderness is the temptation to find a ready-made path that will lead out of it.

But no established path will do.

No religious movement, community, or practice will rescue anyone. All they can do is reassure a person that they will survive the flood even though that person has no convincing way to believe them.

The flood is not the flood if you know you are going to get through it.

Nothing can get you there, and that's because there's no 'you' and no 'there' in the ordinary sense of those words.

We sometimes talked about the variety of Christian movements springing up and claiming special revelation and purpose. There were so many churches with so-called, special end-times mandates.

Have you noticed how everyone in these groups sounds the same? he asked.

Yes, I have, I said. *Like a tribe of orphans who've developed a secret language.*

Some of them even have the same blank smiles and unctuous gazes.

He laughed.

And loads of them are having the same visions and hearing the same things.

Babel, he would say. *Babel, again and again, and until the end.*

What do you mean by that? I asked, once.

All the religious movements, communities, practices, and paths will go the same way. To begin with, they promise a ladder to heaven. Everyone speaks the same language, and all seems clear.

Then what? I asked.

The euphoria can't last forever and then the cracks in the tower begin to show.

It seemed a true enough analysis.

What do you see when you look in the cracks? I asked.

That's a good question, he answered.

He thought for a while and said, *Two things: first off you see the wilderness that's waiting for everyone when they get tired and their cracks begin to show.*

And then? What's the second thing? I enquired.

You realise that all the time everyone was talking the same language they were meaning different things.

- 52 -

The nagging thought that I would never get out of the murky pit I found myself in was a constant threat, whispering in my ear, and it terrified me.

I can't pretend that I ever embraced my descent into the darkness back then, but there did come a time when I began to accept it.

He seemed to pick that up and one day he asked, *So, now you're here, how do you find it?*

I'm not sure, I replied. *It seems as though I can't find anything. Nothing is real.*

Yes, that makes sense, he said. *It's like getting used to walking on water.*

We were sitting at his table, facing each other.

Did you ever think that this is what that story might be describing? he asked.

Jesus walking on the water?

Yes, he replied. *It's a good description of where you find yourself.*

He was looking at me as he continued.

It's actually a good description of where everybody is, but most people never end up looking down at their feet, so they never notice it.

I remembered the story.

When Peter does look down, I added, *he sees there's nothing under his feet to stand on and he panics.*

Harvey was nodding.

He notices what you are noticing, he said. *Nothing is real. Nothing has any substance of its own. Nothing is what it seems to be.*

It made me think of the opening line of the Book of Genesis: "In the beginning God created the heavens and the earth. The earth was without form and void, and darkness was upon the face of the deep; and the Spirit of God was moving over the face of the waters."

Except here it's Jesus, strolling over the face of the waters.

The waters is as good a way as any to describe all this, you know? he continued. *It's a swirling, rushing, flowing, meandering, pooling, destructive, nourishing cascade.*

So many adjectives! I teased. *Now who's the poet?*

He smiled. *Except that what I am talking about isn't a noun, so the adjectives don't really describe it.*

I had a sense of what he was saying but the whole thing brought about a profound sense of vertigo. I was swirling myself.

Does it take long? I asked. *To get used to it?*

There was a warmth and a kindness about him on this occasion.

It took me a long time, he answered.

An easy silence settled over the conversation. I was watching him.

How did you know when it was done? I asked.

When I looked down into the waters and saw His reflection looking back at me for the first time, he said.

His face lit up.

You know what I'm getting at don't you? he said.

Yes, I said. *I do.*

He reached across the table and took my hands in his.

That's when you'll know it's done, he said.

- 53 -

While we are on the subject of the waters and everything that points to, I've always been taken with the story of Jesus calming the storm.

My favorite version is found in Mark's Gospel where it is set after dark.

Jesus tells his disciples that it's time to go to the other side and there's probably plenty enough to be said about that simple phrase and the fact that going to the other side probably always happens in the dark.

So, there they are, bobbing along in the Sea of Galilee, which is really a large fresh-water lake, when a storm hits. It's the same expanse of water that Jesus walks on in other stories. A lot happens on that patch of water.

The boat is hit hard and being swamped with water. His disciples are filled with fear.

He is happily asleep, on a cushion, in the stern.

And then comes the cry that every believer must have uttered for thousands of years when life dishes up a storm of one sort or another and God seems to be nowhere to be found: they wake him and cry out, "Do you not care that we are perishing?"

He doesn't seem to care too much about their distress, but he does tell the Sea of Galilee to behave itself: "Peace! Be still!"

Apparently, the Greek words of the text are better translated as "Quiet! Be muzzled!" It's as though he's addressing an unruly dog.

The dog obeys instantly, and we are told that the winds die down and there was a dead calm. It reminds me of the way Philo always responded to Harvey.

It doesn't say whether he went straight back to sleep after rebuking his disciples for their lack of faith, but I like to think that he did.

And while he settled in for a second snooze, all they can manage to say is: "Who the hell is this? What are we dealing with? Even the wind and the waves obey him!"

My storm was still raging. I couldn't find God, whether he was asleep or awake. I was desperately looking to board another boat.

I was still running from the promises made at my baptism.

Part 2: Purification

I've jumped my chosen ship
a hundred-thousand times.

I've ridden waves and winds
and surfed the shifting sands

of long-too-many empty promises
of mine, time after time after time.

Time to go down with this one
into the nimble, hungry waters,

and watch as their fluid fingers
reclaim what belongs to them.

Long-past time to pay the dowry
I once pledged at the mirror-pool.

Long-past time for the unravelling;
the grave-clothes have become my skin.

Long-past time for the fire of love
and the ruthless kiss of death's release.

Long-past time for him to wake
and take the tempest by the throat.

And all this while he still sleeps like a cat
wrapped in the warmth of his own storm.

I don't know why I showed it to him, but I did. I was past caring about my self-image as a spiritual poet.

You can't write your way out of this, he said.

I didn't reply.

Then, when he'd read the poem, he said, *Yet another story with you as the spiritual hero?*

You're in love with your tragic-romantic self. It's your God.

Speak your mind, why don't you? I said.

You're not expecting anything else, are you? he asked.

I had to laugh.

No. Not really, I said.

Let's go, he said.

Where to? I asked.

The pub, he answered. *That'll knock the drama queen out of you.*

Philo led the way, pulling at the lead. He loved the pub. He could smell the pork scratchings from a long way off.

He'll wake up when you do, he said.

What do you mean by that? I asked.

God, asleep in the stern of your boat. He'll be there, staring you in the face when you snap out of your own dream.

We ordered drinks and settled at our usual table in the corner.

You mean I don't get woken with a kiss, like Sleeping Beauty? I continued.

That would suit you, wouldn't it? he said.

Yes. It would, I answered, before I realised how petulant I was sounding.

He smiled to himself then, in a way I had come to expect when he was about to shatter one of my illusions.

It may yet happen like that, he said, *if you insist on being a child.*

- 54 -

The pain was difficult to cope with, as was the dark, depressive heaviness.

But it was the feeling of being well and truly lost that I found the most unsettling. It's like being suspended somewhere. Or like being caged somewhere that's too narrow to sit and too shallow to stand.

My early evangelical formation had convinced me that God had a plan. It also assured me that my inheritance was so bound up with my vocation, and that vocation was measured by a degree of success in ministry, that they were pretty well indistinguishable.

My earlier Catholic formation should have taught me that it's not the case at all.

It's hard to describe the dying, and so it should be. On some days, my entire body felt like lead. I had no strength. On those days I was a man with no future. Those were days when nothing offered me any comfort at all. They were days when I was sure God had abandoned me, utterly.

You'll know you're deep in it when you are convinced you are a forgotten thing, he said.

Jeremiah's loincloth, I said. *Good for nothing.*

His presence was reassuring, but on bad days I couldn't tolerate any company at all, not even his.

He seemed unflustered through it all.

This has to happen, he would say.

When will it end? I asked one time.

For you, never, he said.

You won't get out alive.

He was smiling as he spoke and that lit a fuse in me.

You're pissing me off, Harvey! I shot back. *You love playing the esoteric smart-arse. I've had enough of it!*

He was utterly unperturbed by my anger and, after a long pause, he spoke again.

I'm not playing games, he said. *This is very serious. Listen.*

He was watching me.

It's a lie that we will all be raised, you know?

No, I said. *I didn't know that.*

I was irritated.

But I've got a feeling you're going to have something to say about it, I said.

There's only One that's ever raised, he said. *Only One. Again, and again and again.*

I listened and watched as he spoke. I couldn't work out whether he was teasing me.

If this is a joke, your timing is pretty, fucking awful, I said.

He found that funny.

I've never felt this low and you are telling me there's no way out?

No, he said. *That's not what I'm saying. What I'm telling you is that only One of us ever gets out.*

I'm going home, I said. *I've had enough of your cryptic bullshit.*

Another tantrum? he asked.

Fuck you!

Listen! he said.

It was whispered and urgent.

To what? I asked. *You screwing with my mind?*

The kernel stays in the grave, he said.[23] *Do you understand?*

I didn't.

The branches stay in the fire. Only the vine emerges.[24]

As I dug for change in my pockets to pay for my coffee, he pressed on.

Only the First-Born opens death's womb.[25]

I left the money on the table, stood, and put my coat on.

Don't expect to do it yourself, he said, as I left.

- 55 -

You're in the Cell of Self-Knowledge, he said.[26]

It's painful. It could also be called the House of Humility.

Part 2: Purification

It had been a very difficult few days.

When it has done its work, you'll be under no illusions about yourself anymore. And when that happens, you'll know everything you need to know about God.

I had read that St Thérèse of Lisieux said it was important to bear serenely the trial of being displeasing to oneself.[27] I was bearing it with anything but serenity.

I was humiliated and angry.

We were drinking coffee at the Crab Apple Café. It was a cold, sunny morning. We were seated outside so I could smoke.

Smoking was just about the only thing I could do.

It's perfect freedom and peace, you know.

What? I asked.

The freedom from all illusions about yourself, he answered.

The charade ends, he continued. *No need for any more pretence.*

I was coming face to face with the charade, and the illusions and shame that brought it to life and continued to sustain it. It comforted me to realise that I was beginning to understand what he was talking about.

That wasn't always the case.

There's only one vocation in this House, he said.

Vocation? I asked. *That's something I'm no longer sure of at all.*

Watching and waiting, he said. *Nothing more than that.*

Later, in the afternoon, I picked up the thread again.

What did you mean when you said that after this was done, I'd know everything I need to know about God?

We had been wandering around the town, talking, for most of the day. We stopped here and there for a smoke or a cup of something.

Well, he said, *in the House of Humility, you confront yourself as you really are. All your wounds are laid bare. All your sins exposed. The structure of your entire personality and the foundations of your very self are excavated.*

I was already confronting the depths of my anger, fear, and grief. My wounds were unavoidable. They stared me in the face.

I nodded. *I am a broken, lost thing,* I said.

That's a beginning, he answered.

We crossed the road by the almshouses and headed for the newsagent. I needed cigarettes.

And if you are finding it hard to look at now, imagine how difficult it will be later on.

You're not helping, I said. *You can be such a fucking prophet of doom sometimes.*

He ignored that.

So, at some point down the line, you'll find out that God doesn't find it hard to look at. We turn our faces away from ourselves all the time. God doesn't.

Screw God! I smirked. *I don't even know what that word means any more.*

I went in, bought and paid for my cigarettes, and came back out. He was waiting, with Philo, on the pavement outside.

It's shame that makes us turn from ourselves, he said. *God is not ashamed, and God does not turn away.*

OK, I said. *Supposing that's true, how does it answer my question?*

It always struck me that he wasn't the least bit intimidated by my anger.

The House of Humility will teach you that there's no such thing as self-esteem. That's a charade too. Perhaps the greatest of all the charades.

How is that an answer? I was getting increasingly irritated and I lit a cigarette.

I need to spell it out, don't I? he said.

Yes. You do!

You'll find out that you don't love yourself at all. That you can't. That no one who has ever been here has.

Fucking hell! I cursed. *Are you going to welcome me to the club? I don't want to join!*

No, he said, smiling. *But I am going to tell you that this is when you'll learn what it actually means that God is love. And what it means to say that he first loved us. You can't know that until you've seen that there's no love in you.*

He stopped walking then, turned and looked at me, and said, *It'll be nice to know that the scripture you've been peddling is true, won't it? Think of it, you won't be a black belt in shabby Christian platitudes anymore.*

As he turned and started walking again, he said, *We've all got that to look forward to.*

- 56 -

It was a few days later and I had calmed down a bit.

We were in the pub.

Self-esteem is the greatest charade of them all? I asked.

I agree, he replied.

I'm quoting you! Don't you remember?

He laughed.

So, you are, he said.

People might say that's your line because yours is so low, I continued.

They might, he shrugged.

Or maybe you're just the world's greatest misanthrope?

He smiled at this. It was almost as though he liked the idea.

Well, he said, *there's no rush is there? You're not going anywhere just yet, so you've got plenty of time to work it out. It's always good to work it out for yourself.*

It was mid-afternoon, and we were alone. We had walked Philo over the hill to the other side of the vale and back and we were thirsty.

Have you got any cigars? he asked.

No, I replied. *Shall I get us a couple?*

It's the least you could do, he said with a wink.

We smoked outside.

Now, he said, *tell me about this self of yours that you would like to hold in high esteem?*

I couldn't really answer that.

I'm not sure what it is, I replied.

Nobody does, he answered, *and yet they want us to have some sort of regard for it.*

I cast my mind back to my teaching days and remembered the times a pupil would ask me to define God. I would often answer with a question of my own: "I'll define God for you if you tell me who you are?"

It's actually a harder question.

It's playing with stories, he said. *That's all.*

What do you mean by that?

If you can cast yourself as the hero in your story then you can call that self-esteem, he said.

Like people who make the victim-to-survivor switch? I asked.

He didn't reply.

There's nothing wrong with reinventing yourself, I continued.

No, he said. *There's nothing wrong with anything, really, though. But why live as an invention?*

I didn't know how to reply to that.

What I am talking about happens when all the stories end. When you discover that you're not who you think you are at all, there's no need to invent a self. No more I am this, I am that, I am the other.

Just, I Am who I Am? I wondered, out loud.

Yes, he said. *But be careful.*

Why? I asked.

Because even I Am who I Am is a story for you at the moment.

- 57 -

I suppose it was only a matter of time before the Archdeacon raised the topic.

I had agreed, reluctantly, to meet with him every once in a while to discuss my options and prospects. I think I was just being loyal to my old Bishop.

It was clear to me that he thought I was going through a psychological episode of sorts and that I needed an intervention. He didn't say as much, but there was a sense that he was reigning himself in. I think he was just deferring to his own bishop who had obviously decided, acting on advice from his old friend, that I was worth the effort.

So, he asked, *how much time are you spending with Harvey?*

He couldn't say the name without betraying both a distaste and a nervousness that ran counter to his usual slick disposition.

When I told Harvey later, he said, *That bloke is smooth enough to make a man feel welcome in his own home.*

I had to laugh at the time but later I came to realise there was a more sinister suggestion in the joke. A man who can manage that can also manage to end up with his name on your title deeds.

You know him? I asked.

That surprises you? he retorted.

Yes, I said. *I had no idea.*

The Archdeacon made it clear that Harvey was considered a loose cannon, and a dangerous one at that. The general message was that I really should be taking spiritual direction from someone more on-side.

Perhaps I didn't give him enough of a signal that I was buying his version of Harvey and towards the end of our meeting he showed his hand even more.

The thing about Harvey, old chap, he put his hand on my arm at this point, *is that it's really all about him.*

His therapeutic, soothing tone unsettled me.

He's a classic egotist and, unfortunately, our profession can be a haven for that sort.

I found it interesting that he described it as a profession. I hadn't ever thought of it in those terms.

He left me with an uneasy sense that I was being managed rather than cared for, but I couldn't shake the suspicion that, in trusting Harvey, I had trusted a man I hardly knew with far too much.

Harvey, on the other hand, made no attempt to manage me at all.

He said you were an egotist and that this whole thing will be all about you, I said later.

We were at his place. He was cooking, and I was opening the wine I had brought with me.

Pour me a glass of that, he said.

He drank, put the glass down then said, *Well, who are you coming here to see?*

You, I suppose. I laughed.

We drank quietly for a while, and he put the finishing touches on some very good, braised lamb shanks.

It won't always be about me, you know. I'm just the midwife. When the baby comes you won't give me a second look, he said.

I didn't know how to respond to that.

He picked up his glass and said, *Let's drink to that good day.*

As he was mopping up the remaining mashed potato and sauce, he said, *Unless, of course, you'd rather put your soul in the hands of our venerable friend?*

No comment, I said.

Part 3: Illumination

Then his disciples asked him what this parable meant. He said, "To you it has been given to know the secrets of the kingdom of God; but to others I speak in parables, so that 'looking they may not perceive, and listening they may not understand.'"

Luke 8:9-10

- 58 -

My heart is broken, I said.

We were walking in the woods.

I know, he answered. *Blessed are those who mourn.*

It was very early in the spring, but it didn't feel like it. Winter was hanging on by the skin of its cold teeth.

I don't know if it will ever heal, I said.

It was getting dark.

Will you manage if it doesn't? he asked.

I don't know, I said. *On days like today, it feels like I might not.*

I called Philo as we turned and headed for his place.

It's on days like this that the oil and wine come, he said.

You know that? I asked.

I knew he was referring to the Parable of the Good Samaritan. It might have been an apt metaphor: I was feeling well and truly battered and left on the side of the road to die. I couldn't find any solace in the Church and had become reliant on a man who didn't seem to fit anywhere.

Yes, he said. *I know that.*

I can't explain how but I think I knew it too.

My anger was slowly abating, and the fear was losing its grip. Despair had turned to something like sadness. My own void, that black hole of confusion, grief, and sorrow, no longer looked like a stagnant, sulphurous swamp from which I would never emerge.

I wasn't even sure I could put a name to anything I might find in there.

- 59 -

I arrived late that night. It was Maundy Thursday, and it was dark and strangely cold for late March.

Sorry, I said, as he opened the door.

What for? he enquired.

I was at the service.

I followed him to his kitchen.

Oh, he said, turning away and back to his cooking.

His fire was roaring, and his place was stifling hot. He was in a T-shirt and shorts.

What service was it? he asked.

Eucharist, foot washing and stripping the altar.

I remember them, he said, as he prodded at a pan in front of him with a long wooden spoon.

He took a taste of the soup he was brewing.

So, did your altar get stripped too, in the process?

What? I asked. I wasn't sure if I had heard him right.

I didn't think so, he said.

The thing is that by the time spring came around, I did begin, very slowly, to understand.

My own altar, that collection of ideas and images that clothed my identity and my world with a sense of purpose and meaning, was well on its way to being stripped bare.

The Paschal Triduum, the holiest three days of the Christian calendar, begins with the liturgy on the evening of Maundy Thursday. It continues through Good Friday commemorations of the Passion and reaches its high point in the Easter Vigil, which is often a late-night Mass beginning on Holy Saturday and ending in the early hours of Easter Sunday.

Outwardly, it commemorates the betrayal, passion, death, burial, and resurrection of Jesus. Inwardly, it asks us whether those events in his life are commemorated in ours.

What goes on outside the church is far more important than what goes on inside her. The fact that Jesus was crucified outside the gates of the holy city is not an idle detail.

This thing is no respecter of so-called sacred space.

The Maundy Thursday service is grounded in Jesus' Last Supper with his disciples, from which our Eucharist is drawn. That's worth remembering but it's the next bit that Harvey was referring to: after the service, the altar is stripped of all adornment. Candlesticks are removed along with all the linens covering it.

All images are, likewise, hidden. The icons and statues are covered in black cloth.

The church is, figuratively, stripped bare of meaning and interpretation for the next couple of days. It remains in this fallow state for the duration of the next day, Good Friday, which commemorates his torture and crucifixion, and Holy Saturday, the day that revisits his time in the grave.

It's a painful, silent time. It's a fertile void.

It's dark and bare and it remains like that until the Easter Vigil, the celebration of the resurrection, begins with candlelight, and meaning and love and light and warmth flood the world again.

And that's exactly where I was. I was still disorientated but I was beginning to get a whiff of its fertility.

- 60 -

You keep referring to God and Jesus as thieves.

Yes, he said. *I do.*

Don't you think you ought to be more careful with your use of words?

Why is that? he asked. *He died outside the city walls and between two thieves because that's where he belongs. You'll never really know God if you keep insisting on his goodness in the way you do.*

You have tamed God and confused that with goodness, he continued. *It's insipid nonsense.*

We were sitting on his sofa, looking out over a herd of cows grazing in the paddock that ran adjacent to one side of his place. They were so close to the house I could almost hear them chewing.

Well, you might put people off, I replied.

That's exactly what I am hoping to do, he answered, with a smile on his face.

He stood and moved to the window. The dog followed.

As his gaze swept across the herd and the paddocks beyond, he said, *The truth is even more unpalatable. God is not just a thief, he's the lowest kind of thief. God is a graverobber.*

He turned back towards me. *The thing is that he steals what was never ours in the first place and he takes it all, including our very selves. We were never ours.*

He laughed at this point and added, *So, you see, I am already toning it down.*

As he headed for his kitchen, he asked, *Want something to eat? I'm hungry.*

I followed him to the kitchen and told him I wasn't hungry.

I've got nothing to say to people who don't long to have their graves plundered, he said.

He put bread into the toaster, took the butter out of the fridge and opened a jar of Marmite.

How can I talk to those who don't even know that's where they are? he said.

He watched the toaster until it sprang.

They will think I'm a lunatic, he said with a chuckle.

- 61 -

Spring was erupting all around. When spring comes it's an explosion.

The spring seems to erupt from innumerable pockets just below the surface of the soil: Lenten roses; snowdrops; crocuses; violets; daffodils; primrose.

It seems impossible after a long, listless winter.

Everything has been lying flat on its back in deep rigor mortis for months, and, when the sun returns and breathes its warmth into the land, those pockets of hidden life stir and tear their way through a grey soil to puncture the fields and woods and gardens with a reckless, elfin joy.

Spring is life in free-fall. It hurls itself carelessly towards death every year, all for the sake of flowering.

Early spring still carries winter's bite in its fingers and toes, though. The ground is still crusted with a cold shell.

My perspective alternated between these two views of the season.

On a good day, the spring bulbs and flowers illuminated my world with the promise of life and beauty. I was beginning to see buds of proof that this darkness would not cover the face of the earth forever.

On a bad day, all I saw was the fragility of those buds. It looked as though they might lose their battle with the icy ground and the numb depths beneath it.

- 62 -

People love the devil, he said.

You're going to have to explain that, I said. *Who exactly?*

Christians, especially, he said. *Too many Christians.*

We were walking Philo. The grass was wet with rain, but the skies had cleared, and the sun shone.

You know, he said, *he's very important for many people.*

I hadn't thought of that, I said.

They wouldn't know who to be without him, he continued.

My mind wandered to think of the countless people, and ministries, engaged in flamboyant, so-called spiritual warfare, and the prayers, in the Catholic tradition, to St Michael the warrior archangel, whose job it is to fight Satan.

The words started to come back to me: "Holy Michael, the Archangel, defend us in battle. Be our safeguard against the wickedness and snares of the devil. May God rebuke him, we humbly pray; and do you, O Prince of the heavenly host, by the power of God cast into hell Satan and all the evil spirits who wander through the world seeking the ruin of souls. Amen."

When a person needs to define themselves as a warrior, he said, *there's got to be an enemy.*

Old Nick keeps people in business, he added.[28] *And more than that, he gives people identities.*

For many Christians, he is actually the father from whom every family in heaven and on earth takes its name.

We let Philo off the lead and watched him run.

They'd be lost without him, he continued. *Nameless.*

It seems like a lot of people are like that, I agreed.

I was lost myself.

Old Nick is the cornerstone in their lives, you know? Not Christ.

So maybe there's something they fear more than him, I said.

Philo was here and there, sniffing out trails.

Like not being anything? I asked. *Extinction. Insignificance. Namelessness. The abyss.*

Yes, he said. *That's it.*

He thought for a moment then, before saying, *It's a shame, you know.*

I didn't reply.

Because that's where their new name is, in that abyss.

- 63 -

As we walked, there was an increasingly easy familiarity between us, but I found myself wondering whether I trusted him.

I couldn't say yes to that without hesitation; there were times he seemed evasive and elusive and I had been inured to suspicion and mistrust from a very young age. I prided myself on being highly sensitive to motives, especially when they were hidden, but with Harvey I have to admit to being out of my depth in this regard.

He was tricky.

You keep talking about this abyss, I said. *It sounds chilling.*

It is, he replied. *You should know. You're in it.*

Yes, but on good days, I am not without hope, I said. *You make it sound worse than it is.*

He smiled at this and we walked on a few paces.

You've only just entered it, he said. *It will get worse.*

I called to Philo, who turned and ran towards us. Perhaps I thought he was better company.

Do you want me to lie to you? he asked.

No, I said. *Don't do that.*

The abyss is also the bridal chamber, the place where the Beloved weds his own, he said. *It's worth it.*

That's good to know, I said.

But that doesn't happen until the abyss is truly that: an abyss, he continued. *The abyss is not an abyss when you can see the bottom of it.*

He could tell, from my silence, that there were times I still dreaded my solitude. I was still longing for an end to this experience of disorientation.

At least you've got Philo, he said. *And me, too. I didn't have anyone to talk to.*

He patted Philo on the head then and whispered to him.

Looking back, I should have had a dog, he said.

Actually, he continued, to Philo, *I should have had a lurcher, just like you.*

Philo was smiling at him.

The lurcher is technically a mongrel. But it's a specific type of mongrel: a sighthound crossed with another breed, often a collie or a terrier of some kind. It looks like something between a greyhound and a Saluki.

The name might come from an ancient Romany word, 'Lur,' which means thief, and 'Cur,' meaning a mixed-breed dog. In archaic English, lurcher is the word for a thief, a swindler, or a prowler.

Historically, it's a poacher's dog, and that's a nice little story because for hundreds of years the English and Scottish governments banned commoners from owning sighthounds, like Irish wolfhounds, Scottish deerhounds, and greyhounds. So, lurchers were bred secretly to fulfil a need.

Poachers worked out that crossing certain breeds with sighthounds produced a more intelligent dog with a better nose and often some herding abilities. They are beautifully adapted for hunting small game.

A lurcher would have been perfect for you, I said.

Why is that? he asked.

Because they're an unregistered breed, I said. *Just like you. The Kennel Club won't have them.*

He laughed and turned to Philo again.

Perfect, he said to the dog as he admired him. *Just perfect. The Kennel Club won't have me either.*

- 64 -

Jesus was a lurcher. He didn't fit.

He said so himself when he told his disciples that 'Foxes have holes, and birds of the air have nests; but the Son of Man has nowhere to lay his head.'

There is a peculiar and painful asceticism in having nowhere to lay your head and it doesn't just refer to where your pillow is. It's not just a reference to homelessness. It's a way of suggesting that we are not granted the luxury of a fixed, stable identity.

We don't have a reference point from which we can look back at ourselves and define ourselves. Christ is often called our cornerstone, and this refers to a Christian conviction that he is the reference point from which we can look back and make sense of the edifice that is our troubling, mysterious selves. But that doesn't really help anyone because Christ is, himself, a mysterious, troubling self.

Ultimately there's no-where to stand. There's no-thing at home in any of us, really. All attempts to objectify ourselves and turn ourselves into some-thing we can point at, understand, and approve of, are destined to fail.

We are lurchers. We don't fit. We will never know what it is, or who it is, that we really are and that's because we will never know what it is, or who it is, that we are talking about when we use the word God.

God is not an object, and neither are we.

God is a lurcher. God doesn't fit.

This painful 'placelessness' is beautifully illustrated in the life of an obscure Catholic Saint, Joseph Benedict Labre, the patron saint of rejects, beggars, the homeless and the insane.

Labre felt an early call to the monastic life but was repeatedly rejected as unsuitable by both the Cistercians and Carthusians before settling on a life of vagrancy. He wandered across Europe from shrine to shrine and eventually died, at the age of 35, of malnutrition in Rome during Holy Week of 1783.

The story goes that when he died the local children took up the cry, 'The saint is dead! The saint is dead!' Well, of course they did: "Out of the mouths of infants and nursing babies you have prepared praise for yourself."

His reputation spread quickly in the city and then the rest of Europe and it was only because of this that his parents heard of the whereabouts of their lost son. He was canonised in 1883.

As Thomas Merton once said, having nowhere to lay your head means that you can't make your life fit in with the books.

- 65 -

A few days later we were at his place, drinking tea.

One of the big temptations at this stage, he said, *is to bail out.*

Bail out? I asked.

Yes, he said. *To come up with a plan that is actually an exit strategy. And the plans that come to us at this point always look good and righteous. It can even seem as though that's what God wants us to do.*

I knew exactly what he meant.

The thing is, he said, *all they offer is an ephemeral promise, but that can make us think they are, somehow, ordained.*

I had been dreaming of a monastery, of late.

You need to know, he said, *that the Phantom will always offer you a way out. It'll tell you that the abyss is nothing but a tomb.*

Isn't it? I asked. I wasn't in the mood for a lecture, however benign.

No, he said. *And the Phantom never sticks around long enough to find out that it's also a womb. This abyss is your grave and your mother.*[29]

He offered me another cup of tea. I could see he was concerned.

Don't bail out, he said. *Don't jump out of the crucible. You'll only have to come back if you do.*

The temptation to bail out was powerful. I would have invented any number of versions of myself, come up with any number of scripts, just to avoid this crushing sense that there was nothing substantial about the entity I had called Me since I was a child.

The only thing I could reliably call Me was a bundle of riotous insecurity. At this stage it was nothing more than a very frightening feeling that there was no Me, against which I protested as though my life depended on it.

It's a strange thing. Me, at its root, exists entirely against a backdrop of its own absence.

- 66 -

He was energised as he spoke but also, somehow, grave, and serious.

The biggest challenge of the abyss is the feeling of insignificance.

That's exactly how I feel, I said.

Yes, he nodded. *And it feels as though it's intolerable.*

It's like I've got no purpose, I continued. *I don't mean anything.*

Hold on, he said. *Be strong.*

We had been talking for hours by this stage and he brewed another pot of tea.

The Phantom will be telling you that the abyss is a bottomless pit to extinction; that there's no way out. It'll be telling you that you got yourself here and you can get yourself out. That your exit strategies will dress you up in the meaning and significance that you crave.

They are all lies.

If they are, I replied, *they're nice lies.*

I remember, he said.

I can't say he was at all comforting but talking to him did make a difference. It was an encouragement. All he did, really, was tell me that I could get through this.

Becoming anything, a monk, a hermit, a mystic, or anything else, at this stage, is just another attempt to rebuild your own temple.

It will fail.

You seem so sure of that, I said.

I'm sure, he nodded.

They are merely stories in which you cast yourself in this or that role.

You will have meaning and significance in the stories for a while until they collapse again and fall around your feet. And when they fall around your feet you will find yourself naked again, which is where you are now, and where you have to stay until he comes.

So just grit my teeth and live in this hole? I asked.

Yes, he said, *naked as Adam.*

You're big into nudity, I said.

He laughed at this. It was the first glimmer of his humour and playfulness in an otherwise intense and serious afternoon.

Naked as Adam, I repeated.

That was his mistake, you know?

Eating the fruit? I asked.

No, he said, *playing dressing up with the fig leaf.*

- 67 -

I still can't believe you had no help getting through this, I said to him one morning.

It was a constant preoccupation.

I didn't say that, he said.

He got up and headed for his bookshelf. There were a handful of recipe books on it, an encyclopaedia of plants, some volumes of poetry, and a bible.

I said that I didn't have a dog and that I had nobody to talk to. But I did have some help.

He handed me a copy of St John's Dark Night of the Soul.[30]

I didn't know you had this, I said.

You might recognise yourself in Chapter 10 of Book 2, he said. *Have a look.*

I did.

He sat in silence as I began to read.

> *"For the sake of further clarity in this matter, we ought to note that this purgative and loving knowledge, or divine light we are speaking of, has the same effect on a soul that fire has on a log of wood. The soul is purged and prepared for union with the divine light just as the wood is prepared for transformation into the fire.*
>
> *Fire, when applied to wood, first dehumidifies it, dispelling all moisture and making it give off any water it contains. Then it gradually turns the wood black, makes it dark and ugly, and even causes it to emit a bad odour.*

By drying out the wood, the fire brings to light and expels all those ugly and dark accidents that are contrary to fire.

Finally, by heating and enkindling it from without, the fire transforms the wood into itself and makes it as beautiful as it is itself."

When I put it down, I looked at him and he asked, *Make sense to you?*

Yes, I said.

When you are here, God always says, 'Let there be dark,' before he says, 'Let there be light.'

He was looking at me, earnestly.

Light is all there is after the dark has been consumed, he continued. *The darkness isn't real.*

That rang a bell somewhere. St Augustine said something along similar lines about evil; that it's nothing but a privation of good. Evil has no substance in and of itself.

Take it home, he said. *It's yours.*

Thanks, I said.

It won't all be helpful, but you might find it comforting to know you're not the only one.

I sat in silence for a while. It was a relief to know there was a community to be found in this black hole in which I found myself.

But what if this isn't God? I asked.

You mean, what if you're insane? he replied.

Yes, I said.

Well, he answered, *only time will tell.*

He had turned away from me and was looking out of the window towards the pastures.

Being mad is somewhere to go, he said. *It's something to be.*

You may prefer it to this nameless emptiness.

- 68 -

Solitude can be a pose, he said.

That made sense. I remembered that the Catholic psychoanalyst, Gregory Zilboorg, had once told Thomas Merton that what he really wanted was a hermitage in Times Square with a large sign over it, saying, 'Hermit.'[31]

It doesn't just mean being alone, you know.

What does it mean, then? I asked.

True solitude means not borrowing anything. No words. No ideas. No practices. No tribe.

Nothing.

I was getting the idea.

Being alone means giving up on the hope that you'll be found because you've attached yourself to something else.

I had tried, many times.

All the while avoiding the gaze of the One whose eyes search our emptiness.

It was beginning to make sense to me. I had borrowed so many faces over the years.

Cue me as saved. Cue me as born-again, I said.

He smiled, *Cue me as sold-out-for-the-Lord.*

Cue me as Bible-believing, Bible-loving, Bible-quoting.

We were going back and forth.

Cue me as the Man of God, he said.

Cue me as the Theologian.

And me as Post-Evangelical, he continued.

And Progressive? Contemplative? Monastic?

Cue me as a Fresh Expression![32] He put a big smile on for this one.

The absurdity of it all made me laugh harder than I remember laughing for a long time.

You? I exclaimed. *A Fresh Expression!*

We walked happily on for a while. The sun was shining, and it was good to be with him.

I feel good, today, I said.

Me too, he answered.

- 69 -

Later, we stopped off at Folio for a coffee and a sandwich.

I couldn't resist my usual browse in the religion section, and I came back to our table with a collection of some poetry by the Sufi poet, Hafiz.[33]

Do you ever read? I asked him as I sat.

No, not really, he said.

He took a sip of his hot coffee.

I did for a long time.

Theology? I asked.

Mostly, he said. *And some other stuff.*

Why did you stop? I asked.

The café was deserted, and Philo was happily settled next to us on the floor.

Too much noise, he said.

He took another sip.

Too much noise about nothing.

I listened, quietly.

There comes a time, he said, *to turn away from an addiction to words.*

The Bible? I asked.

Yes, even that, he said. *Perhaps even especially that. You know it so well by now, it wouldn't hurt you to put it down for a while.*

It felt strange to be advised not to read scripture.

And as for theology, he said, *what makes you think the ideas and words of others will help you in the bridal chamber?*

He started to laugh at this, as though an absurd image had occurred to him.

You'll sound no better than a cheesy pick-up artist if you do that.

We drank in silence for a while until he picked up the thread again.

Is that how you used to get women?

What do you mean? I asked.

By using lines written by others to entrap them?

No, I said, *I was never really one for chat-up lines.*

Really? he asked. *Then what makes you think God is interested in them?*

I'd never heard it put like that before.

He wants to hear your voice, he said.

He turned and looked me right in the eyes, and repeated, *Your voice. Not the borrowed voice of another.*

- 70 -

I had a sense of what he was saying.

Reading can be an addiction. I had escaped into worlds other than my own for so long.

Any world was better than my own, disappointing one. Reading was a way of becoming someone else for a bit. It was a chance to live someone else's story.

By reading, I had often avoided a disturbing question: what was it in me that needed to reimagine itself in the being of another?

He picked up my copy of Hafiz and leafed carelessly through the pages as my own thoughts ran away with themselves.

Listen to this one, he said. *This is something worth reading.*

> "When no one is looking,
> I swallow deserts and clouds
> and chew on mountains
> knowing they are sweet bones!
> When no one is looking
> and I want to kiss God,
> I just lift my own hand to my mouth."[34]

His whole face lit up as he read. His eyes looked like fire. It made me nervous.

That's surprisingly good, he said.

It's audacious, I said.

Yes, professor, he mocked. *It sure is.*

I'll write you an essay, I said, joining in with his parody.

I was used to his teasing by now. I also knew he considered my intellectualism to be a defence.

You'll miss the point in an essay, he said. *That poem contains everything there is to contain.*

How is that, then? I asked.

You'll find out what he means when you know that no one is looking.

That stopped me in my tracks.

I was coming to terms with the unsettling truth that I had always played to an audience.

Everything I had ever done had been in the hope of being seen. Of being noticed and celebrated.

Hafiz doesn't even watch himself, Harvey continued. *Can you do that?*

No, I said quietly. *I can't.*

Let's talk when you can, he said. *Then you'll know it's not audacity and maybe you'll be able to write the essay.*

That is true solitude, he added.

It's the place where things are hidden since the foundation of the world.

- 71 -

I finally began to see what Harvey meant when he said that I was devoted to, what he called, my project.

I had spent most of my life devoted to it.

My project had never included the possibility that no one might be looking. My project was all about being seen. Somewhere, not-so-deep in the recesses of my psyche, I was always planning for fame. I longed to be celebrated, and to be honest, it didn't much matter what for.

Anything would have done.

When Harvey suggested that the freedom I was looking for happened in secret, when nobody at all was looking, I found myself utterly without motivation.

The depression hit hard. What was the point?

My project, my own Tower of Babel, was born of a desperate hope and fuelled by a gnawing desire for a certain kind of revenge. The hope was a fragile one: that I wasn't as insignificant as I feared I was. The desire for revenge by succeeding was a sad and very common one: I wanted to show them, whoever they were.

To see myself, in my mind's eye, as successful, as celebrated, was to refute and triumph over the voices that whispered insistently that I would amount to nothing.

Let's be plain: I was hard in pursuit of an idol and running from ghosts.

Harvey's freedom from both my preoccupations was clear to me from the very beginning. Perhaps that's why I found him so compelling.

You'll learn, in time, to love being invisible, he said.

I doubt that, I answered. *I'm far too insecure.*

He laughed at that and said, *There's a remedy for that too, you know.*

Oh? I asked. *Let's hear it then.*

Being misunderstood, he answered. *And learning to live with it.*

- 72 -

Gloom, I said.

Yes, he replied. *That's what happens when our projects begin to die.*

He was gentle. Almost reassuring.

No shadows, even, I said.

A tomb? he asked.

That might describe it, I answered. *Loss and grief, too.*

You're saying goodbye to your life's work, he said.

What do I do? I asked.

Nothing, he said. *Nothing at all.*

I found that unbearable.

Be empty-handed, he said. *There's nothing you can bring to this.*

As we walked, I was overwhelmed with a sense of my own emptiness.

I have nothing, I said. *I am nothing.*

He nodded.

I pulled a piece of folded paper from the inside pocket of my coat. I had been writing and it seemed to me to sum up my plight perfectly.

> My stories are gasping for
> breath - those words with which
> I enchanted my worlds.
>
> These myths, these veils
> in which I clothed a hero I could
> never find, have crumbled.
>
> Letter after letter falls from
> all my horizons' hopes like rain
> that's nothing else but rain.

He smiled and said, *I don't like it much. But at least the spiritual hero myth is dying.*

Shall we take poor-old-you to the pub? he asked with a wink.

OK, I said.

We walked almost all the way there in silence. His company was a comfort to me.

Just hold still, he said as the pub came into view.

Hold still and you'll see someone else flowering where you used to be.

That just sounds like empty words to me today, I said.

Yes, he said. *But they're true words. I promise you that.*

The time will come when you don't need to write yourself into existence anymore.

- 73 -

The most difficult thing to face up to, was the growing realisation that, in my own project-devoted mind, I had, for too many years to remember, enlisted God as my second-in-command.

I prostrated myself for years before the image of my future success. I expected God to prostrate himself, alongside me.

More than that, I expected God to arrange an occupation for me that would conjure up the kind of recognition I was longing for. I should have had the self-awareness to see that my entire spiritual life was, secretly, a desperate and repetitive incantation: Make me great. Make me great. Make me great. Make me great…

Actually, it might even be more poignant than that. The incantation might be: Make me real. Make me real. Make me real. But that's for another time.

When I started to realise it was never going to happen, a cocktail of shameful emotions bubbled to the surface: frustration, rage, despair. I caught myself sulking.

He must have picked up on my state of mind when he suddenly said, *Love.*

What? I asked.

Love, he said. *Just love, that's all. It's the beginning and the end.*

It's no fucking use to me! I answered.

I lit a cigarette. I was agitated.

I'm so lost that I can't see the end of my own nose and you're getting sentimental?

He sat quietly for a while as I smoked. He was watching me. When he did speak, it was quiet and reassuring.

None of us really know it's the answer until it comes, he said.

It was a word that didn't mean much to me at all, truth be told.

I had always been suspicious of claims to love. It seemed to me that most of the time it was an attempt to enlist cooperation in someone's agenda. I had done it myself: for years I had assumed that if God loved me, he would, at the very least, grant me what I wanted.

And now, with my own spiritual pretensions unveiled and my own agenda unravelled, the last word I was ready to use about anything was love.

And yet I will show you the most excellent way, he said.

I didn't answer but I knew he was quoting St Paul.

I've got to go, I said, suddenly.

I was angry and frightened of what I might say or do to him if he pressed on.

Bye, he said.

As I turned and walked away, he called after me, quoting the Song of Solomon, *Daughter of Jerusalem!*

What? I asked, as I turned.

Do not arouse or awaken love until it so desires.

Fuck off, Harvey! I shouted.

As I strode off, I could hear his laughter ringing in my ears.

The strange thing was that I wasn't being mocked. It was the infectious, joyous laughter of a child who knew that something wonderful was on its way.

I know birth pangs when I see them, he said, the next time I saw him.

- 74 -

There's an old saying, beloved of certain spiritual types, the enlightenment chasers: when the student is ready, the teacher will appear.

When this student was not ready, Harvey came along.

Harvey wasn't a teacher in the ordinary sense of that word: he was the proverbial axe, laid to the root of the tree.

He was a demolition expert, something like blind Samson in the temple of Dagon.[35]

Do you know what kind of monstrous strength it took to topple those pillars? Only a blind man with nothing left to lose except his hair is capable of that kind of ruthlessness.

No one with a reputation is qualified.

Harvey undermined my columns, tore down my walls and stripped the altar.

It's your god that keeps your You in existence.

I agree with that, I said.

We were having tea.

I don't think you get me, he said.

I drank more tea.

What did you mean, then? I asked.

Well, I didn't say that God keeps you in existence. God wants you to die. But first he needs you to kill him.

It had always perplexed me that the fountain of God's love, according to the Christian story, was prized open by the most iconic moment of violence in history: the torture and the murder of the innocent man, Jesus of Nazareth.

What is it that makes us think that violence was perpetrated by others on our behalf?

Worse still, what allows us to think that the slaughter might even have been arranged by God?

How easy it is to locate our own malevolence in others.

How perverse to locate that malevolence in 'god' and then prostrate ourselves before an idol we can only ever pretend to love because it is pregnant with the possibility of our own degradation and torture.

To call this worship is to confuse an act of reverential love with an act of timorous, self-abasement that is not worthy of the name.

To corrupt an old proverb: better the god you think you know than the God you know you don't.

That's what spiritual poverty is: admitting that you don't know what you pretend to know at all.

- 75 -

We were talking about scripture one day.

All that bible-reading! he said. *It'll do you no good until you plough it, you know.*

Plough it? I asked.

Yes, tear the top crust and rip it up into furrows.

I don't know what you mean, and even if I did, I wouldn't know how, I replied.

He was looking at me intently at this point, before he said, *The kingdom of heaven has suffered violence, and the violent take it by force.*

So now you're a bible-basher! I said, laughing.

I'm very serious, he said. *Don't be frightened.*

Frightened?

Yes, frightened, he repeated.

Until you see that the Mark of Cain is written on your own palms, you won't find the treasure in the field.

Now it just sounds like you're playing the arcane guru, I said.

Or, maybe, you're just confused, he answered, *because that's easier than finding the violent man.*

A curious silence filled the room, and I had the strange sense that he was saying something true and significant, even though I had no idea what he was talking about.

OK, I asked, *show me how to plough.*

I am, he said. *We're ploughing now.*

- 76 -

Like its master, the scripture must be subjected to an act of violence before it can release its chrism.

Nothing much nourishes us until it is picked, shelled, peeled, burnt, or in some way violated. That's as true of the holy text as it is of food.

The words and stories must be allowed to collide with each other. Contradict each other. Interrogate each other. When they are bruised and battered beyond the recognition of our ordinary ways of thinking, they can become the salve they were always intended to be, without us knowing it.

We've got to break and spill the text, just as we break the bread and spill the wine of the Eucharist before it can heal us.

We need to be encouraged to desecrate the text so the text, in turn, can desecrate us and lay bare our pet notions of God, which can only ever be idols.

Harvey said, *Jesus spat in a man's mouth. He also spat in a man's eyes. And you're complaining that my words are offensive?*

As long as we insist on reading it in the ways we have been taught that it ought to be read, then we are, by definition, engaged in a fearful, and fruitless act of mimesis. This is the imitation of men, not the imitation of Christ who did violence to the text in the name of love again and again.

Harvey called it ploughing the scriptures. It was a game he loved to play.

One day, while we were walking, I asked him, *What's the worst advice you've ever been given?*

Touch not the Lord's anointed, he said.[36]

Why is that?

Because I did, he replied.

And did you die?

Yes, he said.

Any regrets?

No. Not at all, he said.

How so? I asked.

That's the way I found out He was the gate.

Another time, at his place, I asked him again, *What's the worst advice you were ever given?*

Not to eat the fruit of that tree.

The Tree of Life?

Yes, he nodded.

Did you eat?

Yes, I did.

Why? I asked.

Because He told me to, he said, with a gentle smile on his face.

And on another day, while he was cooking, he said, *It's all about the fruit.*

What? I asked.

The fruit of the first tree closed the gate. The fruit of the second tree opened it.[37]

I don't get it, I said.

If you don't get it, then stop saying that He is the way and the truth and the life.

He went back to his cooking for awhile and I watched his back.

When he turned away from the stove with two plates in his hands, I sat and waited.

Words are not food, he said, as he slid my plate in front of me.

- 77 -

Paradox is the Golgotha on which the ordinary mind is crucified.[38] The mind of Christ lies on the other side.

We are supposed, as Christians, to be able to live with the nourishing uncertainty of paradox. Most of us can't. We tend to bear down on one side of the paradox in order to confirm our bias.

For example, from the early Christological insistence that, in Jesus, humanity was confronted by a being who was fully God and fully human, the Christian tradition has emphasised his divinity over and above his humanity. It is perfectly orthodox to say that in Christ God became a man, but we struggle with notions that Jesus was a man who became God.

The Church is often pretty quiet on the teaching of one of its own Fathers who said that God became man that man might become God. It's not a sermon you hear preached very often.

The so-called Christology of descent has trumped the Christology of ascent. Why?

Harvey would say, *Follow the money.*

When you've built an organisation on the foundations of a sacramental theology that insists that the church is the channel and source of grace and salvation, and you've developed a priesthood ordained to minister those sacraments by virtue of the dubious claim that they are signed with the special character of Christ the priest, it's important to emphasise the divinity of Christ.

The same goes for another paradox: the Christian insistence both on God's transcendence and immanence: God is inaccessible, above and beyond the material world, but; God is also accessible, present, and dwelling within the material world.

The transcendent has taken priority and the church has made sure of it. The church has set itself up as the mediator, the channel by which the transcendent makes its way into our hearts and minds.

For the church, the immanent is something to be controlled and named and located in places defined as sacraments, or doorways to the sacred. Where they acknowledge God's immanence, they make sure they are the guardians and gatekeepers of it.

God's immanence, God's intimate, indwelling of all there is, might just lead a person to realise the implication of that astounding claim: our very being is nothing other than God, who inhabits everything, including us.

It might not be accurate to say that, by virtue of God's immanence, everything is God. It is accurate, however, to say that God is everything, as well as being the source from which everything arises.

There is only one being in the universe and that is God.

What use for a priesthood to minister, like some parsimonious accountant, the treasures of grace to a people whose very being and life force is none other than the presence of the God they claim to deputise for?

St Catherine of Genoa puts it like this: "My me is God: nor do I know my selfhood except in God."[39]

St Paul tells us this plainly when he says that we are the bearers of treasure in jars of clay.

The church has convinced us to pay them interest on our own treasure.

But I didn't know that then.

The rascals, Harvey said with a smile. *Jesus said he was the gate and they have set up a toll booth.*

He chuckled. *The shameless rascals.*

There was a hint of admiration in him as he spoke. It confused me because I thought it looked like the secret pride of a father who cannot resist the naughtiness of a wayward child.

Don't you care about the people who are duped by the Church? I asked.

It takes two to do that dance, he said. *They need each other.*

My censure was something he didn't trust or believe.

Why do they piss you off so much? he asked.

I'm not sure, I answered.

Is it because you care about people? Or is it because you fell for it for so long and you feel foolish? he pressed.

I think so, yes, I said. *The latter.*

Then spare me your confected, righteous indignation, he answered.

It's tawdry.

- 78 -

Spring was well underway. The magnolia trees looked like giant candelabras.

We were stood, admiring one when he asked, *When you were training, what did they teach you about preaching?*

Lots, I replied.

Too much then, from the sound of things. Did any of it help? he asked.

Some of it. Mostly it was a chance to practice and get feedback.

In the silence that followed, I cast my mind back over numerous lectures and workshops.

Did they teach you that the art of preaching is the art of grave robbing? he pressed.

No.

Then they let you down, he said.

There was nothing to say.

The tree reminded me of an immense menorah, and that led me to wonder what Moses may have felt like as he stood in front of the burning bush. I had no urge to take my shoes off, but I carried on savouring the spectacle.

It must have seemed odd to any passerby; two men and a dog staring up at the branches and flowers of a tree.

The blossom would soon be gone.

They should have taught you to preach, he said, again.

They did, I protested.

I turned towards him. *What are you getting at?* I asked. I was irritated.

There were homiletics courses and assignments throughout.[40]

At this he convulsed with laughter. It went on until I interrupted.

Where did you learn it? I asked.

Not there, he chuckled.

I didn't appreciate his attacks on my training any more than I appreciated his cryptic games.

You can't preach until your own veil has been torn, he said, suddenly serious.

After a pause he continued.

Then you get to tear the veil yourself.

- 79 -

His garden was newly tended. The soil had been dug over and enriched, and little signs of green were coming through in rows: chard and spinach, broccoli and kale, beans and peas.

Have you read the story of Legion, the Demoniac?[41]

Yes, I replied. *Many times.*

We headed back indoors. It was chilly.

You relate to it?

We got to his kitchen table and sat, facing each other.

In many ways, yes, I do, I said.

I watched him as he drank from the cup in front of him and then placed the cup back down on the table.

Do you relate to it? I asked.

Yes, he replied, *but it's no longer my story.*

What do you mean by that?

Well, he said, slowly, *I am still living in the tombs but there's no demoniac there anymore.*

What's there now, then? I asked.

Just the treasure He left behind after he plundered the tombs, he answered.

He refilled his cup from the pot and asked if I wanted more tea.

- 80 -

I think Samson was his favourite character in the Old Testament. I used to tease him, saying that he had a 'Sam-sonic' ministry.

Samson has long been considered a type-of-Christ. He who destroyed the temple of Dagon foreshadows the man who said: "Destroy this temple, and in three days I will raise it up."

Except for his prowess with women, he replied. *That passed me by.*

Shame, I said. *A good woman would have knocked off your gnarly edges and taught you some manners.*

He smiled at that. He wasn't in the least perturbed.

Well, I would have been no use to you in that case, he said. *You're so stubborn that you needed to collide with a greater force than your own.*

It was true. I did.

He went back to Samson.

Your favourite topic, again? I asked.

Yes, he replied. *Samson knew what it was.*

Knew what? I asked.

He stopped to think for a moment, then said, *Knew what it was to suckle nectar from the slain.*

I wasn't sure what he was referring to.

'*Out of the eater came something to eat. Out of the strong came something sweet.*'

Are you quoting scripture at me? I asked.

I knew the story: Samson slays a lion on his way to meeting a young Philistine woman he fancies, and days later, when he walks past the carcass again, he notices that bees have set up a hive in it. Honey flows from the dead body of the lion and Samson scoops up a handful and eats it.

Yes, he said.

When you slay the lion, you'll know too.

- 81 -

When I talked to him about my dormant priesthood, he was always evasive.

I think it might have been your last-ditch attempt to find a costume that fit, he said. *A last grasp at a face you think you might be able to live with.*

I was trying to work out whether a role like that was ever going to be a part of my future.

How long before you realise that you'll be better off naked? he asked.

Later, when the pub had filled, he asked, *So, have you found your face yet?*

What do you mean by 'my face'?

Why don't you know that? he asked. *You're a priest and you don't know that?*

There was a lively buzz in the place, and Philo had been joined by a couple of other dogs.

I think I have an idea, I said.

Go on then, he said. *What do I mean?*

The beer had loosened the conversation a bit and he was playful and combative.

Something about showing myself, I answered, *and using my words?*

That's something like it, he smiled. *Show it! Even though it's pain-riddled and you can't stand the sight of it yourself. Even though it's been hidden for so long now that you don't even know it's you.*

I drank more of my pint.

Philo looks so happy in the pub, I said, changing the subject.

He looked around, taking in the other dogs. A Jack Russell sat attentively on a bench next to his owner and a large mastiff was sprawled across the wooden floor.

I do love a pub dog, he said.

We sat in silence.

Shame, he said, abruptly. It was a strange way to begin a new conversation.

Shame? I asked.

Yes, he said. *It's shame that stops us from showing our faces.*

That makes sense, I said.

I knew, first-hand, how painful an experience shame was.

The thing is, he said, *that you'll end up discovering another face.*

Another face?

Yes, he answered, calmly. *The face you show now is only the one you think you have. But you can't shed it until you show it.*

He finished his pint, asked if I wanted another, and headed for the bar.

- 82 -

I saw him again a few days later.

I wanted to know more about his thinking on faces.

It's just a metaphor, he said. *A way of talking about identity. That's all.*

Maybe, I answered. *But it sounds a whole lot richer and more poetic than most ways of putting it.*

True, he said. *But don't let that seduce you.*

We were at his place, in his garden. It was the middle of April.

I had brought a couple of good cigars and we smoked as we drank his beer on the deck in the late afternoon sun.

What did you mean when you said I would discover another face?

Just that, he said.

He smoked quietly for a bit, then added, *Just that. You'll end up discovering that your real face is not quite your own.*

You mean like a shared face? I asked.

Something like that but it's older than you are, he answered.

Older than you, too? I asked, with mock incredulity.

Piss off! he said, as he smiled.

I was happy, there, sitting next to him in the warmth.

Older than anyone, he said. *Before Abraham was, I am.*

He reached down to pat Philo. The dog's brindle stripes shimmered in the sun.

But you've always known that, haven't you boy? he said.

His garden was already productive.

He was scanning the rows of vegetables as he said, *It's the Church's biggest lie, you know?*

What is? I asked.

She doesn't mean to tell it, of course, but maybe that makes it even worse.

What are you talking about? I persisted.

She shouldn't be pretending to see when she doesn't.

I stopped pressing for clarification. I could see he was on a roll, consumed by his own thoughts.

The fact that she offers nothing with such confidence is worrying.

He was getting to the end of his cigar.

It means she is focussed on her own rhetoric.

Oh dear, he said, as he stubbed his cigar out and frowned. *These get pretty toxic when you get to the bottom.*

He took a drink of his beer and carried on. *How she can lay claim to any authority when all she offers is presentation is beyond me.*

I smiled to myself, wondering when he would realise that I wasn't following anything he said.

Shall we make something to eat? he asked.

That would be good, I said.

Before he got up, he looked at me and said, *She hasn't yet realised that her true face is not her own.*

Really? I said.

Yes. Really, he replied. *If she did, she would stop offering change. She would stop letting people think they could become better. More holy.*

Are you speaking for everyone? I asked.

He didn't respond.

It's the Church that has given us the Gospels that you refer to so much. And the poet and the mystic you gave me to read.

He ignored me for a while before picking up his train of thought again.

You know that this is what transfiguration is, don't you? A change of face?

That's an interesting thought, I said.

I remembered from my school days that 'figure' was one of the French words for face. I also remembered the stories of Moses and Jesus whose faces became something other than faces and shone like the sun.

The Church needs to make sure she's not telling people they can make the old face prettier when what they've got to find is a new one.

He got up and headed for his kitchen.

That's what it means to be born again, he added.

Philo and I followed.

- 83 -

There was still something going on inside and around me that I didn't understand.

The certainty and joy of my early Christian life was a thing of the past, as was the confidence I once had in the so-called communications that would come to me from the divine. Any sense that I was being guided went out of the window.

My attempts to read St John of the Cross had been of some comfort to me in this new stage but there was always a nagging sense that what I was actually doing was dressing up a nervous breakdown as something spiritual.

St John warns that 'melancholia' might be at the root of the experience I found myself in. I think it might be his word for clinical depression.

When Harvey handed me his copy and suggested I might relate to the image of the fire and the log, it marked a turning point.

St John says that one of the worst torments a person suffers at this time is the deep sense of isolation: "Wherefore, it is a difficult and troublesome thing at such seasons for a soul not to understand itself or to find none who understands it."

Looking back, I now wonder why it's so difficult to find others in the same boat. I wonder how many people are passing through this Night without being able to talk to anyone about it? Maybe that sense of falling apart, the fear that our centre will not hold, is too shameful and frightening to admit to?

After all, it's not an easy boat to pilot.

And then, of course, there will be the multitude of the well-meaning. St John warns about them again and again.

They're often the first to offer to pray. The first to offer advice: "For some confessors and spiritual fathers, having no light and experience concerning these roads, are wont to hinder and harm such souls rather than to help them on the road."

Their sense of their own ministry compels them.

Harvey used to say, *Watch out for those with callings and their milky looks. You'll end up as a sideshow in their ministry games.*

St John of the Cross compares them to Job's Counsellors: "For it will come to pass that God will lead the soul by a most lofty path of dark contemplation and aridity, wherein it seems to be lost, and, being thus full of darkness and trials, constraints and temptations, will meet one who will speak to it like Job's comforters, and say that it is suffering from melancholy, or low spirits, or a morbid disposition, or that it may have some hidden sin, and that it is for this reason that God has forsaken it."[42]

They're full of the self-assurance of those who haven't yet had a good look at the abyss within, so, as a result, aren't afraid to rush in where angels fear to tread.

In other words, they haven't got a clue.

- 84 -

We ordered a couple of pints and the usual pork scratchings for Philo and sat.

So, he said, *you've read some St John of the Cross and now you're preaching on it because you're a qualified mystic?*

We were in the pub.

A note of sarcasm? I asked.

Yes, he nodded. *A hefty note.*

I took a drink from my pint.

So, you've found a new fig leaf to wear? You can play the contemplative now? That must be a relief.

I had to admit that I had latched on to the teachings of the great mystic. I also had to admit that it had provided an anchor for my chaotic spirit in the middle of all the darkness.

Is playing the contemplative game any better than any other? he asked.

I could feel a sense of embarrassment rising. It was as though a charade I didn't even know I was playing was being uncovered.

He opened the pork scratchings and gave some to Philo before picking out a bit for himself.

I can't stand contemplatives, he said.

As he chewed the salty, crispy rind, and followed that up with a long drink of his beer, he continued, *I've never met a contemplative who's comfortable in the pub.*

They're not dressed for it. They take themselves far too seriously.

I could feel a mounting hostility as he spoke.

You gave me the Dark Night to read and now you're ridiculing me for it?

Yes, he said. *I am.*

Why? I asked. *Just because you feel like being a prick?*

He laughed.

It was as though moments like these were the ones that he treasured the most. They were the moments, often when my anger flared up, that I was at my most vulnerable.

No, he said. *I gave it to you because I thought you might find some comfort in it. Not so you could redefine yourself as a mystic.*

I knew he was on to something, but I didn't have a clue how to respond to him. I felt like a fraud.

It's just borrowing another set of clothes that don't belong to you, he said.

He got up and asked if I wanted another pint. I didn't. My glass was still half full.

When he got back to the table, he took a pen out of his coat pocket, turned a beer mat over and started writing.

Here, he said, when he was done. *Wear it around your neck with pride.*

I took the mat from him, turned it over and read: **DO NOT DISTURB – MYSTIC AT WORK.**

It was written in large capitals.

- 85 -

The next time we met, he was in a less ruthless mood.

Contemplation has become fashionable, he said. *There are contemplative teachers gathering tribes of little contemplatives who all sound like them.*

He was shaking his head.

When folks outgrow their evangelical clothes, they often adopt contemplative ones, thinking the new costume is, somehow, better than the old one. Both are worthless rags.

We were walking, in town.

The whole point of the fire is that it burns off the old rags and reduces any new ones to ashes too.

This seems like a hobby horse of yours, I said. *And it seems like a high horse, too.*

It is, he said. *The whole thing pisses me off.*

It always struck me that he never tried to hide his anger. I had spent a lifetime denying mine.

I waited as he chose and bought some sausages from the butcher.

The venison ones, he said. *A dozen, please.*

He picked up the theme again as we left the shop.

If there is such a thing as contemplation, or mysticism, it's nothing more than sitting in the fire and letting it burn all costumes off. It's got nothing to do with a sexy little set of spiritual practices and the oily jargon of mystical-speak.

Nudity again? I chuckled.

He laughed.

St John of the Cross talks about it too, he said. *All the time. He calls it denuding. So, how anyone can read him or quote him and think he's offering them a new set of clothes is beyond me.*

I was beginning to understand, even though the humiliation of the previous conversation still stung.

Want to know the Gospel according to St John of the Cross? he asked.

Go on then, I said.

Get your kit off, he said.[43]

And that's it.

- 86 -

There were days of joy and wonder. Days when I marvelled at the work being done in me.

But the dark days were terrible, and they got worse.

I remembered Harvey's familiarity with the Gerard Manley Hopkins poem, and I began to understand it, intimately. This movement between the burning and the relief: "More pangs will, schooled at forepangs, wilder wring."

In the early stages, I could convince myself—on days when I felt more grounded, more solid, more real than I had ever remembered feeling—that the work was done. But I came to realise that more pangs were on their way. The early burnings were preparation for more, as the fire reached deeper and deeper.

And so, it went, back and forth and on and on.

Hopkins' eloquence astonished me. How does a man find words like these: "Woe, world-sorrow; on an age-old anvil wince and sing"? How did he know?

Because he had been roasted and battered and stretched and shaped on this age-old anvil too.

Long before I ever got there.

- 87 -

The hardest part is giving up all plans, I said.

He nodded.

I've got none, and the ones I had are all dying.

He was watching Philo as I spoke, but I knew he was listening, carefully.

I'm marooned. Stranded.

Philo was wandering here and there, sniffing at whatever caught his attention.

Abandoned.

He looked up then, and said, *You've been praying for this for years.*

I didn't understand.

"Thy Kingdom Come, Thy Will be Done," he recited.

I had never thought that my present crisis could be an answer to prayer.

That prayer needs to be prayed carefully, he said.

If people knew, they probably wouldn't pray it so easily.

- 88 -

I'm so lost.

He was walking next to me.

Lost. Lost. Lost. Lost. I kept chanting the word.

There was a degree of comfort in repeating the truth.

Completely. Fucking. Lost.

He held the lead and Philo ambled happily between the two of us.

There are no words to describe this.

No, he agreed.

He was sombre, and I could see that he knew what I was talking about and shared in my pain.

No moorings, I continued. *No maps. No direction. No foundations.*

Nada, he said.

What? I asked.

St John of the Cross, he said. *Nothing.*

Yes, I affirmed, *Nothing but nothing. No connections. No signs. No omens. No lights. No stars.*

St John covers it, he said.

> "In order to arrive at that which thou knowest not,
> Thou must go by a way that thou knowest not.
> In order to arrive at that which thou possessest not,
> Thou must go by a way that thou possessest not.
> In order to arrive at that which thou art not,
> Thou must go through that which thou art not."[44]

You know it by heart? I asked.

Yes, he said.

It doesn't help, I said. *It's no use trying to sketch me a map using him. Where there are no words why would I borrow those of another?*

He laughed then and put an arm around my shoulder.

Touché, he said. *You're getting stronger. But don't let that little victory distract you.*

You're nearly there.

- 89 -

Later in the spring, he asked, *What will happen to you when you find what you are looking for?*

We were walking Philo in the meadows and sat, for a while, on a bank while he paddled and drank deeply from the stream.

What do you mean by that? I asked.

Well, he said, *you've been a seeker for so long you might not be able to be anything else.*

Like a finder? I mocked. *Whatever that means.*

It means something very real, he answered gravely.

The meadows were full of dogs and walkers and Philo was full of running and play.

The seeking game is very addictive, and you've been playing it for so long, he repeated. *How long is it?*

About thirty years, I said.

He nodded to himself and seemed deep in thought.

We stood and made our way towards the gate and the road beyond.

Finding is the end of all games, he said. *It will break your seeker's heart.*

That sounds painful, I said, as I put the lead on Philo and he opened the gate.

It is, he said. *Until the seeker is well and truly gone.*

Then what? I asked.

Just the Beloved, he said.

Nothing else but the Beloved.

- 90 -

I read something interesting a while ago, I said. *It was by Harry Williams, have you heard of him?*

No, he said.

He said that "Religion is to a large extent what people do with their lunacy, their phobias, their will to power and their sexual frustrations."[45]

He smiled and thought for a while, before asking, *Do you count yourself among them?*

Sometimes, I said.

We were at the pub. It was mid-morning and a weekday, but he decided he wanted a pint.

Does it matter, he asked?

We spent a lot of time at the pub.

Does what matter? I enquired.

He lit a cigar.

What people do with their lunacy? he replied.

The smell of his freshly lit cigar filled the little alcove in which we were sitting, and the rays of sunlight played with and through the smoke.

They've got to do something with it, he continued.

I suppose that's true, I said.

We sat in silence. I felt awkward and he was watching me intently.

Feeling empty-handed? he asked.

If you're asking whether the silence makes me uncomfortable, then yes, I suppose it does, I replied.

He laughed then.

Don't worry, he said. *Conversation is to a large extent what people do with their lunacy, their phobias, their will to power and their sexual frustrations.*

You can be such a prick! I said.

This made him laugh even more, and then he said, *It's true, you know. There are lots of ways in which we keep the lunatics at bay.*

As he offered me a cigar, he said, *Go on. Have one. Offer God some incense. It's better than religion and conversation.*

I lit up and inhaled the smoke.

- 91 -

What happened between you and the Archdeacon? I asked, one morning.

An awful lot, he replied.

He ruined my life.

That sounds dramatic, I said.

It's perfectly true, he replied.

It was one of those days when I needed to be in his company.

I had woken feeling isolated and lost and headed to his place before dawn to find the lights on and him awake.

He was pickling green beans. His kitchen table was covered with half-pint jars. Each one contained a peeled clove of garlic and a sprig of dill. A mix of water, distilled vinegar, and salt was simmering in four different saucepans on his stove.

A steamy, acerbic cloud hung in the room.

Utterly ruined, he continued.

Never-to-be-rebuilt-ruined, he said, rhythmically.

He seemed unperturbed as he spoke.

I didn't know what to say.

Will you make us some coffee? he asked. *I've got to prepare some more jars.*

I filled and boiled the kettle, put coffee beans in the grinder, and set out the coffee pot and a couple of mugs.

I thought you were friends? I asked.

We were, he said. *Close friends. But I was a friend who saw something I shouldn't have seen.*

What did he do? I asked.

Nothing, he replied.

I was confused. *Well, what did you see, then?*

He thought for a moment before he answered.

His emptiness.

What does that actually mean? I couldn't picture it.

That's something for the Archdeacon, he replied. *It's not something you need to know.*

There was a finality to the statement, and I knew better than to press the point.

A little later we were sitting at the table. He had taken the apron off.

Why do you seem to be OK about it? I asked.

Because he did me a big favour, he answered. *Not that I knew it then.*

He smiled to himself. *He who finds his life will lose it, and he who loses his life will find it.*

I would never have had the courage to ruin my own life, he added.

It was a great kindness.

Part 4: Union

The kingdom of heaven is like treasure hidden in a field, which someone found and hid; then in his joy he goes and sells all that he has and buys that field. Again, the kingdom of heaven is like a merchant in search of fine pearls; on finding one pearl of great value, he went and sold all that he had and bought it.

Matthew 13:44-46

- 92 -

And the theology degree, he asked, *how was that?*

I enjoyed it, I answered. *Very much.*

After the prohibition on thinking in the evangelical church, it was a welcome change.

He was watching me.

And I had some questions that I needed answers to.

Like what? he asked.

Like how the death of a man a couple of millennia ago changes everything, I answered.

The evangelical conviction that Jesus' death somehow changes God's attitude towards humanity and opens the faucet of mercy for us, didn't ring true.

I remembered reading something by the great Quaker theologian Rufus Jones.[46] In effect, you cannot believe in a God who requires sacrifice in order to forgive those he claims to love and at the same time believe in Jesus' teaching in the story of the Prodigal Son.

You have to choose, and my studies gave me the chance to do that.

And did the degree answer your questions?

To a level, I said. *But all it really provided were elegant explanations and I needed more than that.*

He nodded.

So, after being trapped in the sentimentalism of charismatic Christianity you found yourself trapped in the intellectualism of theology?

I suppose that could describe it, I answered. *And the vanity and rivalry of the professors didn't help. There was more showing-off in the lecture and seminar halls than any catwalk or bodybuilding gym I can imagine.*

The intellectual snobbery was startling.

Phrases came to mind. There was the repeated compulsion to let students know that Kant had to be read in the original German.[47] There were pet put-downs, like, "He's the type of man who quotes Nietzsche without having read him." And there was a deeply held and reflexive distaste of anyone who actually believed in God and claimed to have experience of the divine.

That was clearly, unforgivably stupid.

Their political convictions didn't help either, I continued.

Oh? he enquired. *How so?*

Well, I answered, *it became pretty clear, pretty quickly, that liberal-leaning essays would score you more marks.*

Part 4: Union

He laughed.

Don't tell me, he said.

What? I asked.

You played that game like a master, didn't you? You told them what they wanted to hear.

Yes, I said. *I did.*

He laughed again.

So, you didn't really do your degree to answer some pressing questions, did you?

I didn't say anything.

You were looking to do well. Whatever that means.

- 93 -

It was a Friday in early summer, and we were walking Philo.

Summer always seems to me to be effortless. Spring churns but the summer breezes. After the heroic labour of spring, summer leans back and slides downhill.

The gardens are dazzling. Roses keep on blooming and the cosmos, crocosmia, iris, dahlias, and red-hot-pokers, not to mention the others that I can't name, are in full swing.

It's quite a display.

The wisteria blossoms hang like grapes and the buddleias are festooned with butterflies and bumble bees, and everything seems to drift, like they do, from sweet thing to sweet thing.

This is nice, he said, as we meandered around the town and slowly looped back on ourselves to head for his cottage.

On the way back to his place, he said, *So many of the churches don't know what they are doing.*

Well, that's a pretty thoughtless generalisation, I replied.

It was a beautiful, sunny day and we picked our way through the woods.

I mean it, he said, after a few more paces. *There are so many blind-leading-the-blind that they have become ditches. It's a great shame.*

The sunlight played in patches on the ground, illuminating the ivy, ferns, and redcurrant.

Philo ran ahead.

The ones that are empty are ashamed of God and can't understand why people aren't queueing up for their substitutes.

Substitutes? I wasn't sure what he meant.

They peddle equality, inclusion, and love while their hearts rage with envy, superiority, and bitterness.

Are you having a bad day? I asked.

I still didn't feel comfortable with his attacks on the Church.

No, he replied, quite calmly. He didn't seem agitated.

The ones that are full can't understand that the prosperity and the spiritual power they are selling will end up making everyone crazy and sick.

We reached a clearing and stopped to catch our breath.

It might be right to call God our servant in certain situations, but he is never a servant that makes us fat.

He looked around the clearing.

I'm in search of a good walking stick, he said. *I'm looking for hazel.*

As we walked on, he continued, *Neither is he the kind of servant that trusts his greedy children with firearms.*

- 94 -

The Archdeacon was trying to get me involved in some initiative or other.

The diocese had adopted a so-called missional strategy and decided that this was to be the Year of Hospitality.

Yes, they really said that. Exactly that.

It was straight out of the Archdeacon's playbook. It made me cringe.

It reminded me of the Church of England's ineffective Decade of Evangelism in the 1990s that did nothing to stop the steady haemorrhaging of the bums that were supposed to be parked on the pews.

The haemorrhaging continues.

That sort of strategising has been labelled Functional Atheism by a bunch of people who study these things. It describes an addiction to planning, and, while it makes much of God's involvement, it betrays a fear that if we sat still, did nothing, and waited for God to act, he wouldn't be there at all.

I think it's also got more than a touch of magical thinking about it: if we just come up with the right plan, God is bound to follow us and bless us. If the spell is performed correctly and the incantations are recited word-perfect, the blessing hoped for here is an increase in numbers.

It all puts the ongoing existence of the Church front and centre. The word for that is ecclesiolatry.

I've never been comfortable with such things.

I was even less comfortable with the Year of Hospitality because it exploits a primal and profound human instinct for connection and employs it in the service of recruitment.

My guess is that people don't buy into these things because they know they are being manipulated.

The hospitable people in the diocese were going to keep on doing what they always did because it was second nature to them. They liked people and they enjoyed spending time with them. It was those who weren't naturally gregarious that I felt for. Parishes were being enlisted in all sorts of events and congregations were being pressured into bringing their friends to the various showcases: barbeques and movie nights; children's fun days and makeover sessions for mums.

It was more an advert for the community than the God who might be the reason for the congregation in the first place. And Christian communities are just like any other, with one exception: the obnoxious, competitive, abrasive element can often persuade itself that it has God's mandate for its modus operandi.

I also felt for the local vicar. In a rural diocese like this one, vicars are often overseers of multiple churches; ours looked after five. She was under pressure from dwindling congregations to come up with ways and means of breathing life back into a church, whose only realistic option was closure.

She was also too busy, often attending to the demands of a family who wanted a baptism, wedding, or funeral in a small village church that hadn't been viable for decades because there was a family connection to the place. And there was all the rushing from meeting to meeting and service to service.

She seemed more like a curator of old buildings than someone employed in the care of souls.

So, what are you going to do? he asked with a mischievous smile.

I'm not sure, I answered.

He was enjoying my obvious discomfort. I didn't want to be enlisted by the Archdeacon, but I knew that I would be closing a door to future possibilities in the Church if I refused to participate.

He's not the only one scheming then?

What do you mean? I asked.

The Archdeacon, he replied. *He's not the only one plotting, is he? You're playing a long game too.*

We sat in an awkward silence.

What do you want to do? he asked after a while.

Well, I said, *I don't think I want anything to do with it.*

So, you have your answer then, he declared.

Whether you listen to it is another matter altogether.

- 95 -

And priesthood? he asked, finally. *What took you there?*

It was a long process, I answered.

Can I have a short version of the story? he asked with an impish grin on his face. *I prefer your short stories.*

I got there through the back door, I said.

How do you mean? he enquired.

Well, my theology degree led to teaching for over a decade and by the end of it I was tired of teaching the thing exclusively as an academic subject. I was looking to communicate and live my faith in some way, so I took a job as a lay chaplain.

And that eventually led to ordination? he asked.

Yes, I nodded. *And that led me into parish ministry, which, I think, I had always wanted to try.*

But you didn't last long, did you? He was looking me square in the eyes. *Why was that?*

I looked away.

It's difficult to put into words, I replied. *I had a nagging sense that we weren't doing what we were supposed to be doing.*

What do you think churches are supposed to be doing? he asked. *Playing at community and liturgy? Social work?*

No, I answered. *Not at all.*

The cure of souls, I continued. *Isn't that the traditional way of expressing it?*

Ah, yes! he enthused. *The good-old-fashioned cure of souls.*

I knew I was being set up.

Good answer! he applauded, sarcastically.

And how did you expect to cure souls when yours was still so sick?

- 96 -

My soul is mute, I said.

Is she barren or mute? he asked.

I had to think for a while.

Mute.

As we walked on, I watched the dog catching sight of something and darting in through a clearing in the blackthorn hedge to the left.

All I hear is groaning.

She's in pain? he asked.

Gnashing and weeping, I replied, nodding.

As the dog caught up with us again, panting and smiling, I continued.

But it's not just pain. It's grief and loss.

He was unusually attentive.

It's also convulsions. Like labour.

He seemed to be nodding as I tried to explain.

She's making a pearl, he said.

It was true.

As the oyster slowly laid down layer-upon-layer of its nacre in a silent, laborious passion of its own, things began to take shape.

It was out of focus. It was opaque. But I was beginning to see. I was beginning to know.

But it's not the kind of knowing that is usually associated with that word. It doesn't make sense in any of the usual ways that we measure intelligibility and coherence.

There's a wonderful story from the Desert Fathers that makes the point eloquently. St Anthony wanted to check the understanding of a bunch of monks who came to see him. Among them was an old man called Joseph.

Anthony suggested a text from the Scriptures, and, beginning with the youngest, asked them to comment on the meaning of the text. Each gave his opinion and to each one Anthony said, "You have not understood it."

Finally, he said to Joseph, "How would you explain it?" And Joseph replied, "I do not know." Then Anthony said, "Indeed, Joseph has found the way, for he has said: 'I do not know.'"[48]

It's a knowing in the biblical sense. It's not knowing about, it's knowing, plain and simple, like you might know a lover.

This knowing is self-evident. It doesn't need to explain itself. It knows that it knows, and it knows intimately.

Part 4: Union

- 97 -

In this dark, silent furnace there comes a point when you realise that your history is giving chase.

Any hope, and there isn't much of it, lies in the still-small sense that it will have to open its jaws and let go of you at some point.

There's a growing awareness that this love, this fire, cannot be extinguished. She will not be silent. She cannot be defeated.

Your history, like Pharaoh's army in pursuit at the Exodus, tires. Its voice struggles to be heard above the murmur of the parted waves, and its whispers, once so persuasive, begin to subside.

Harvey used to say that there would come a point where my story would end. I could feel that beginning to happen.

Perhaps this is what is meant by eternal life? A life uninformed by conditioning.

When our history loses its grip and no longer defines our relationship to the present moment, all is liberty and space and freedom.

The past no longer matters. It doesn't need to be resolved anymore.

The future, which was always nothing more than a metronomic interplay between fantasies of triumph and disaster, evaporates. It is, and remains, unwritten.

All there is, he said, *is what is.*

I didn't understand that for the longest time.

And what is, is love.

Preach it, Brother! I said.

Fuck off! he answered, with a smile on his face.

I knew it was affectionate.

You'll know what I mean when you run out of strength for good, he said.

Until then your mind will be writing story after story, script after script.

- 98 -

There's an intriguing verse in the Book of Genesis about a man called Enoch. It has always fascinated me.

It's a small fragment from what is an entire chapter devoted to a genealogical record from Adam to the sons of Noah. This is what it says: "Enoch walked with God; then he was no more, because God took him."

Nobody knows where Enoch went.

It was preceded by a period of mourning, but by mid-June I couldn't find myself anymore either.

What led up to that was a period I can only describe as a dying.

The Me that I had struggled with so much, and for so many years, was also a Me that I was deeply attached to and had grown very fond of. There was an intimacy and a familiarity in it.

It was as though an image of myself, that I had generated and through which I related to the world, was fading. The Me character in my story was expiring and I couldn't find anything to take his place.

That sounds disturbing, but it wasn't. It was a relief.

Those painful feelings and anxious thoughts that had kept me so chained to a sense of self somehow resolved. They didn't make it out of the void.

Actually, it goes far deeper than that: those feelings and thoughts are the very sense of self that is uniquely human and so problematic.

The Me that agonised over the past and was driven, by those wounds, to fantasise over an ideal future, simply ceased to exist.

Whatever or whoever I thought I was became an irrelevance.

Who am I talking to, then? he asked.

I don't know, I answered.

He laughed.

Who am I talking to? I put the same question back to him.

I've forgotten, he said. *A long time ago.*

That was another lifetime.

- 99 -

I remember my first ever conversation. I don't remember how old I was, but I couldn't have been much more than three years old.

Conversation was something adults did for fun but, on that day, it was something I began to enjoy. I talked to a fellow pupil in the kindergarten and it left a profound impression on me. It was my first memory of being a person, in my own right.

I speak, therefore I am.

So, when I lost my sense of self, not only did I lose my own particular way of locating myself in the world, I also lost my voice. There were no symptoms. No pain. No inflammation. I simply couldn't speak. No sound came from my mouth.

Part 4: Union

He was delighted when I told him, in writing.

Hallelujah! he exclaimed.

When he stopped laughing, he poured us tea.

I pulled a poem from my pocket and handed it to him. It expressed the sense of wonder that accompanied the bewildering sense that I couldn't find myself anymore. There was no one home.

> What is this vast,
> edgeless Life, that
> sees from behind
> my blind eyes?
>
> It stands still and
> watches as I drown
> in the murmurs
> of my own hunger.
>
> When I'm gone, its
> smiling face calls
> me the peace that
> passes understanding.

I'm not reading that, he snapped as he handed it back to me.

You just don't know when to shut up, do you?

- 100 -

I always ran from judgement. Why stick around when you know you will be found wanting?

Even the word had the power to send my soul fleeing for the hills.

It happened in July. It was mid-morning.

It was a sultry, oppressive day for summer. The humidity was ripe for breaking with a good spell of rain.

He told me I was brittle.

You've got to man-up, he said. *You're a spiritual milksop, that's why so much offends you.*[49]

And you sound like a playground bully with prayer beads, I answered.

This is not a game, he said.

He seemed weary.

Your one-upmanship is a vain, empty frivolity.

Ouch! I parried.

There you go again, he said. *Grow up or you'll never find out that the crucible is a bridal chamber.*

It was the first time I ever got the feeling he was bored. It worried me.

Before he left, he asked if he could take Philo with him for the day.

It reassured me that his rejection wasn't permanent, and I said, *Sure. Going somewhere nice?*

Just a long walk, he said.

He stood and put the lead on the dog.

I could use the company, he said.

Will I see you tomorrow? I asked.

Yes, he replied. *I'll drop him back early.*

Stand up and be strong, he said, as he walked away. *This judgement is, and can only ever be, a promise.*

Philo didn't give me a second glance.

Judgement and love are not reconciled; neither does the lion lie with the lamb, he continued.[50]

When he was about twenty paces away, he turned, looked at me and shouted: *Judgement is love. The lion is the lamb.*

And then, everything collapsed.

- 101 -

How can anyone say anything about this?

Somewhere,
Between God's face and mine,
life's wings always shimmered,
as though for the first time,
uncrushed.

This happy riot. This spectacle. This incomprehensible display. This beauty, ever ancient and ever new.

This is wisdom: the condition of seeing. It can't be thought. It can only be seen and the seeing is not done by anyone that can think about it.

- 102 -

I'm not here.

To borrow from St Paul, who wasn't here either: It is no longer I who live, but it is Christ who lives in me.

The Bible warns us that no one can see God and live.

Words run away here. They are sent packing. How can I put this? I woke up this morning to find that I'm a guest at a party inside my own house.

But that's still not it. Words go mad here. They know they are not. I woke up this morning to find that I had gate-crashed a party that was mine all along.

This can never be it. The words point at themselves and chase their own tails. I woke up this morning: I've been throwing a party that was never mine to host.

That's more like it but I'm still nowhere close. The words, like me in my dark-vestry dream, are defrocked, so they run back to the party.

- 103 -

There's nothing here and everything is here. Everything is this and this is everything. Everything is singing. Everything is alive. Everything is life.

The Psalm puts it beautifully because it knows: "The pastures of the wilderness overflow, the hills gird themselves with joy, the meadows clothe themselves with flocks, the valleys deck themselves with grain, they shout and sing together for joy."

Every category dissolves. Every distinction evaporates. The lamb is the lion and the lion is the lamb. Above is below and below is above. In is out and out is in. Here is there and there is here. Spirit is flesh and flesh is spirit. The sacred is profane and the profane is sacred.

The veil is torn, and everything is closer than a brother.

St Augustine says that this is more inward than our own inwardness.[51] Everything welcomes us home. St Paul writes that the whole of creation groans in expectation for the manifestation of the children of God. That groaning turns to a cacophonous choir of joy and chants: "He's home! He's home! He's us! He's us!"

On this, the empty
underside, all the
created things are
closer than a husband.

Closer even than my twin,
and I am taken for a wife,
by everything, now that the
window of the heart is clean.

Everything that gives me
birth, before the minutes
and the seconds, smiles
at me and seeks my hand.

I am endlessly betrothed,
to my own face, my own
face is yours and yours

is mine–I am home.

- 104 -

But that, like anything and everything we say at this point cannot be true because there's only One thing at home.

God is the only One here.

God's is the only face, and everything is the face of God.

God has been playing hide-and-seek with God's self!

I walk and as my
tired feet kiss this
holy ground God treads
on his own ecstatic face.
Because he has found me.

As I cup my hands
and lift this water
to my face, God tastes
his own love from my lips.
Because I have found him.

- 105 -

I had been carrying a dead man around for years! I had been listening to the Phantom!

Spiritual practices are useless because they seem to suggest that there is a need for us to get somewhere. They seem to promise a ladder that will transport us from one state of being to another.

The more sophisticated versions suggest that what is needed is a practice that will help us to accept reality as it is. These will teach us to stay in the present moment or attend to the, so-called, 'isness' of things.

It's sophistry. If there's no-one here to climb the ladder, how can there be anyone here to practice acceptance?

There isn't a church in sight, let alone a sacrament. Everything is a sacrament. Everything is the Real Presence.[52]

The church has been selling us our birth-right! We have been paying for our own inheritance!

This is more than laughing.

- 106 -

This is the Body of Christ.

This is the secret identity promised in the book of Revelation: "To everyone who conquers I will give...a white stone, and on the white stone is written a new name that no one knows except the one who receives it."

We are not who we think we are. Everything is the Beloved; everything is the First-Born of all creation; everything is Christ. Therefore, we are the beloved; we are the first-born; we are Christ.

The great kenotic Christian hymn of Philippians is true for all: all creation is the divine emptying itself, endlessly, and moment by moment. God is born, again and again, in order to die, again and again, in a great, self-emptying eucharistic dance of virility and reckless delight.

This is where the unmanifest takes form.

All this?
Can't you see it?

This is how the invisible
wears clothes and the
ineffable sings its songs.

And you?
Can't you see it?

This is where the
incorruptible gets sick and
the immortal tastes death.

- 107 -

But this is also where the immortal knows that death is not.

There is no death because that which we think dies never was. That which we think dies was only ever an idea and ideas are not reality.

That which truly lives was never born, and it can never die. It is the I Am.

This is the One who hovered over the waters. This is the One who was before Abraham was born. This is the One into whom Enoch dissolved.

This is the One about whom nothing can be said. This is the One about whom everything must be said.

I've noticed that I only
ever know I happen
after I have happened.

My worlds are made
entirely of words, of
nothing more than naming.

What is it after death that
will know that it has come?
What is it that will name him?

Death be not proud! You're
just another way of saying
that knowing comes after living.

- 108 -

This display is, simultaneously, a great, paternal silence. A stillness. A rest.

A nameless ground through which, and with which, and in which, everything lives and moves and has its being.

About this great silence, nothing can be said that makes any sense.

This silence is a
newly ploughed
field of whispering

It is trees cooking
and warm bread

falling into night.

The honey of it all
is rock-solid as the
ever-pouring sounds.

This vast chorus
never sleeps—it is
where death, lives.

- 109 -

Then it rained.

All the day long and softly.

There was nothing to do but leave the windows open and listen to its murmurs. I watched it from the shelter of my barren kitchen.

Later, there was nothing to do but walk, silently, in it.

So, I did that.

It fell, patiently, like a day-long dusk, in whispers, tumbling naked from the low, chalky grey of a blurred sky.

Later there was nothing to do but sleep through it.

So, I did that.

Part 4: Union

- 110 -

Early the next morning the sun shone, and he returned with Philo.

He had been poaching.

He held out a couple of large, plump rabbits to me and then, quite suddenly, said, *Something's happened. What happened?*

The banks burst, I replied.

It was all I could think of.

Oh, he said.

He looked unimpressed.

Is that all?

It's enough, I said.

I wrote this, I said, handing him a piece of paper. *It's something like this.*

> When the warmth came
> I knew I knew his face.
>
> I'd been avoiding his
> gaze in my old mirror

for years—from the
very beginning—before

faces came to mean
what they came to mean.

And now he pops up
everywhere—he is the

invisible dressed up
the voice with which

the ineffable seduces me
everywhere and whispers:

The patch has torn its cloth
and the wine has burst its skin.

I don't fit and neither do you.
I never will, and neither will you.

He was smiling as he got to the end of the poem.

I don't mind that one, he said. *They're getting better. But remember not to set up shop around your experiences.*

Then he turned to Philo and tickled his ears.

You don't deserve this dog, he said. *He doesn't know what to do with something like you, does he boy?*

The dog cocked his head as Harvey spoke to him.

You should have seen him, he said. *Those rabbits didn't stand a chance.*

When he looked up at me, all he said was, *You need to run him. He needs to hunt.*

I had never seen Philo looking so happy. He couldn't take his eyes off Harvey.

Shall we cook up the rabbit? he asked.

Sure, I replied. *Good idea.*

Let's do it at mine, he said. *Your kitchen barely manages a cup of tea.*

It was true.

We'll pot-roast it, he said. *I know an old recipe with cider and bacon and mushrooms. And lots of thyme. It's good.*

It was the only thing he said on the walk from Forge Lane to his cottage.

Philo walked next to us, off lead. I looked at him as we walked, and my heart was filled with love and gratitude.

- 111 -

When love comes like a thief in the night, binding the strong man, it all changes.

The crucible is lit like a sanctuary, loss becomes the surest of guides. Pain is a pledge, a promise, and the reminder of a soul, ravaged.

The dereliction is unspeakably beautiful. Lilies flower in every torn corner. The world is populated by angels and enemies become benefactors.

Alpha and Omega turn to each other because all is well.

It took you a while, he said. *I knew it would come, but I was getting tired of waiting.*

I laughed. I think I would have got tired of waiting for me, too.

I couldn't resist a retort, though: *Daughter of Jerusalem,* I said.

This made him smile and he finished the verse that had so enraged me earlier on, *Do not arouse or awaken love until it so desires.*

Shall we go to the pub? he asked.

Why not, I answered.

It was late summer, and as we walked down the alley to the pub, the warm evening air was full of the scent of jasmine, honeysuckle, and roses.

I love to see climbers on old brick walls. At the end of a summer day, the hot bricks seem to intensify the smells and blend them into an exquisite, aromatic cocktail.

Let's get cigars on the way, he said.

I followed as he turned towards the high street and headed for the newsagent's.

He bought a pack of Villiger's and some matches.

I'm going to miss you, he said, as we neared the Pub.

I know you will, I said.

We drank summer ale that night and stayed well after closing time.

I didn't realise this place did lock-ins, I said, as we left.[53]

They all do, he said.

You'll find out now that you're a guest and no longer a customer.

- 112 -

All my worries evaporated. The anxieties about my future, which had looked so bleak, receded behind a thick, warm veil. The veil was alive.

Peace posted like an army of sentries. Peace in front. Peace behind. Peace below and above and all around. St Patrick's Breastplate.[54]

He smiled when I told him.

Yes, is all he said.

There wasn't much more to say.

It's easier to speak of hell, isn't it? he said.

Much, I answered.

I wonder why that is? I mused.

We were sitting by the river.

When the food comes, he said, *there's no need for the menu.*

The taste eclipses the descriptions, I added.

Yes, he said.

Now that you know it can we not talk for a bit? he asked.

Sure, I said.

So, we sat, for a long time.

It was dark when we made our way back to the town. I turned down Forge Lane to mine without saying goodbye. He just walked on.

My heart sang all night.

I read the Song of Solomon: *I slept, but my heart was awake. Listen! my beloved is knocking.*

And the Song was all true.

- 113 -

Peace of mind and so much more.

What passes understanding is the peace of heart. No more grasping heart. No more hungry heart. Heart fed milk and honey. Weaned and still. I'm sure mine purred.

No more longing for an imaginary future: all the idols smashed by the beautiful violence of this peace.

Do you sometimes feel as though you can reach out and touch it? I asked him.

Often, he said, simply.

And I can smell and taste it, I said.

Yes, he said. *Me too.*

I wonder if the Manna tasted like this, I said.[55]

Every biblical analogy I reached for seemed to make sense and to come true, even though all they could ever be are shadows of the reality. The incense and anointing oil; frankincense and myrrh; aloes and cassia; warm bread and sweet wine; the rose of Sharon and the lily of the valley.

The temple was quiet and there was silence in heaven.

- 114 -

I got hooked on silence.

I would sit, at home or on some bench for hours, and just watch the world, myself included, happening.

The only ones who didn't seem puzzled by the spontaneous joy that erupted in laughter, again and again, were Harvey and Philo.

It was staggering.

This gift, this open secret that I had been searching for, for so many years, lay right in front of my nose.

Actually, it's closer than that. St Francis, I don't know where, once said something like: What you are looking for is looking out of your own eyes.[56]

At night I would dream and awake to a feeling that the dreams weren't mine. They originated somewhere else.

During the day I was filled with a realisation that I, myself, was being dreamt from somewhere other than myself.

I was watching the divine play, aware that I was just a character in it myself.

And this is meekness: knowing that your face is not your own. And this is inheriting the earth as it is promised to the meek: knowing that every face is yours.

Knowing that my lifelong striving to become a somebody was a waste of everybody's time, especially mine. But there was no regret, just more laughing.

Just an immense relief and a mirth that I cannot describe.

- 115 -

As I got stronger and began, slowly, to feel as though I might be able to articulate some of what had been happening to me, an invitation to preach came in. It wasn't one that I could realistically turn down.

Perhaps it was the Archdeacon's way of working out whether there was any way I was going to be of use to him and to the diocese. I was still wondering, myself.

What are you going to talk about? Harvey asked.

Not sure yet, I said. *I've been given the Ephesians reading on the whole armour of God.*

You know the one? The belt of truth, the breastplate of righteousness, the shield of faith, the helmet of salvation, and the sword of the Spirit, which is the word of God.

Oh God! he said. *You poor man!*

I laughed at that, before saying, *I've no idea what I am going to say.*

They will be hoping you remind them that the Gospel is going to make them impenetrable and invincible if they get it right.

I suppose that's always the danger, I said.

Well, you could always use it as a way of bursting that bubble, he said. *There's nothing like a bit of holy subversion.*

That's your speciality, I answered. *I wouldn't know where to begin.*

He chuckled.

Except for the story of David and Goliath, I said, a moment later.

Go on? he asked.

Well, David refuses Saul's armour, doesn't he?

Yes, he said.

He was smiling.

It was only a flicker, but I could have sworn a look of pride crept across his face.

Because it wasn't his and it didn't fit, I continued.

There are lots of people wearing armour that isn't theirs and doesn't fit, he said.

I had tried on lots of different armours myself. They didn't help.

Armour becomes a big problem when you realise that the enemy is within, he said. *Because it just fortifies the city, and he can run even more rampant.*

And all the while the city thinks it's safe, I said. *And the watchmen noisily point to threats from the outside.*

I remembered a verse from the Gospels: *There is nothing outside a person that by going in can defile, but the things that come out are what defile.*

There you go, he said. *If you can preach to me, you can preach to them.*

It's easy with you, I said.

Oh? he said. *Why is that?*

Because you're not fortified, I said.

- 116 -

I realised that I was beginning to sound like him.

That didn't, in itself, worry me, but it did make me think. I wondered whether the similarities I noticed came about because I was imitating him or whether I was, genuinely, beginning to discover that he and I were alike.

It didn't matter.

As we continued to discuss Ephesians and the whole armour of God, I wondered what would become of our relationship in the long run.

He broke the silence.

You could also remind them of something very important, of course.

What's that? I asked.

That the greatest battle ever fought was waged, and won, naked. The only armour in sight belonged to those who hung Him there.

I'm not ready to adopt your obsession with nudity yet, I said, with a smile.

Shame, he said. *It would suit you, especially if you grew a long beard to preserve your dignity.*

Like a modern Basil the Blessed? I asked.[57]

Isaiah did it too, he said. *He spent three years naked.*

I'd like to have seen that.

A wicked grin spread over his lined face.

Imagine their faces if you pulled that stunt on Sunday?

The thought did amuse me.

It would be career suicide, I said. *But what a way to die!*

Yes, he answered. *Maybe that's just what you need.*

- 117 -

The sermon didn't go down well.

The convention in parishes is that there are members of the congregation who will always come up to the preacher after the event and offer congratulations or observations. Often, they just want to demonstrate that they have understood something or to offer the benefit of their own knowledge. Most of all it's a chance to connect with a preacher.

My sermon was greeted with an awkward silence. No one connected. No one said a word.

Anyway, with my attention liberated from my own confusion and pain, I began to notice that Harvey looked older than I had thought.

It was good to lift my eyes from their usual focus, but the sight that greeted me when I did, unsettled me: In just under a year, he had slipped from looking like the most vigorous, robust sixty-something that I had ever known, to a slower, more careful seventy-something.

Only his silver-blue eyes betrayed the fact that he still had the energy to shine a forensic light on the lingering spiritual assumptions that continued to comfort me.

As I started to get more involved in local ministry, I wondered again why he never seemed to go to church.

There's nothing there I need to hear, he said. *Why are you going?*

It's what I do, I said. *I suppose I have to go. And, deep down, I care about the church.*

He didn't reply. It was as though he was waiting for more from me.

And I think it matters.

As I began to falter, I noticed what I didn't say with any confidence: that I was going to church to encounter God and learn something.

He didn't pick me up on it.

I'd rather go to a pub, he said. *That's my parish.*

You're sounding like a sad old soak! I laughed.[58]

It was a cheap shot, and I knew it. I had never seen him drunk.

Want to know why I like it better than church? he asked.

Go on then, I said.

Because the congregation in a pub know they are descendants of those who murdered the prophets, he answered. *They might even be drinking because they can't stand the sight of Abel's blood on their hands.*

It was early evening in late August. There was a sense that the summer was burning herself out. Dusk was still a couple of hours away, but the nights were getting longer.

Talking of my congregation, he said, *shall we go to the pub?*

I liked the idea.

On the way down to the town, he picked up the theme again.

It might be your job to minister in a church, he said, *but it's not mine.*

I didn't say you had to work in one, I answered. *I just asked why you didn't go. That's all.*

I don't belong there, he said, simply.

My home is outside the walls, he continued, *with all the other bastard children.*

Now you're sounding like a drama queen, I said.

He laughed.

You're addicted to your feral self.

Touché, he answered.

Hoist with your own, self-righteous, petard, I added.[59]

It was fun turning his own logic back on him. He didn't seem to mind it in the slightest.

We arrived, with Philo, to a happy crowd. The evening sunshine was bathing the tables and chairs outside and a steady hum of conversation and laughter filled the air.

I ordered our usual pints, and we drank in silence for a while. I liked being with him.

Yours is a harder job than mine, you know? he said.

What makes you say that? I asked.

When I confront my congregation with the tombs of the prophets, it breaks their hearts, he said. *They know they took part, so they drink to forget. And my work is to draw near and dissolve them.*

Don't you mean absolve? I asked.

No, he smiled. *You should know that by now.*

And mine? I asked. *What's my job?*

Well, yours are more likely to organise a working bee to decorate the tombs.

You're full of clichés and stereotypes, I said.

There's plenty of truth in some of those, he answered.

We sat quietly for a moment before he continued.

You can't dissolve yours.

Why not? I asked.

They will insist that you absolve them, and then they won't even let you do that, he explained, *because you've got to get them to look at the blood on their hands first. And all the while they will be trying to get you to notice the decorations on the tombs. You poor sod.*

Christianity might just be decorating.

There seems to be a pronounced difference between the religion of Jesus and the religion about Jesus which developed in his wake and became Christianity in all the formats we are familiar with: from the elaborate rituals of the more ancient, sacramental churches; to the modern-day vestal virgins of the evangelical churches, singing Jesus-is-my-boyfriend choruses.

It's easier to worship him than to follow him because following him means dying before you die.

And that means killing Him and acknowledging that.

I knew he had a point, however clumsy.

- 118 -

Just ask poor, blind Father Job.

Remember the story?

God has allowed Satan to afflict Job.

Satan obliges with considerable style: Job's children are killed because the house in which they are feasting collapses on them; his herds of livestock are all taken by raiding Sabeans and Chaldeans; his servants are all butchered by the marauders and whatever is left is consumed by fire from the sky, which also roasts all his remaining servants.

The job on Job is not, however, quite done yet: he is also blighted with painful, running boil-like sores from the soles of his feet to the top of his head.

Job is accompanied by a fickle, nagging wife and a few friends who turn out to be false comforters. They actually believe that he is his own worst enemy and that some hidden sin is the cause of his distress.

He is utterly isolated in his ordeal. No one believes in him.

When Job is at the height of his troubles, he says this: "Though he slay me, yet will I hope in him."

A remarkable show of piety and of what the Bible calls steadfastness.

In this, I suppose, Job is a type of Christ. No matter how bad things get for Jesus he never seems to abandon his hope in God.

Jesus trusts in His God through death and into the beyond: "You will not abandon me to the grave, nor will you let your Holy One see decay."

There is also, of course, a difference. Jesus didn't think God was doing the slaying: "Then Jesus said, 'Father, forgive them; for they do not know what they are doing.'"

Job did, and the book also goes along with this view.

That's why the book is lacking. It needs the New Testament to come along and correct its myopia.

It's always us who do the slaying. God is always the one who is slain.

So, here's what the venerable Job should know now: Though I slay Him, yet will he hope in me!

We know what Job and the rest of the great Patriarchs, as well as the angels, could never know: that we are loved by a God who loves his murderers!

O Felix Culpa! Oh, happy fault![60]

What love is this? A love that no human being could comprehend until Jesus whispered his words of love to us: Though they slay me, yet will I love them. Though you slay me, yet will I love you.

St Matthew's Gospel puts it beautifully: "But blessed are your eyes because they see, and your ears because they hear. For I tell you the truth, many prophets and righteous men longed to see what you see but did not see it, and to hear what you hear but did not hear it."

We see it. Job couldn't.

It's enough to make the most brittle heart melt and sing a song of gratitude and wonder.

Part 4: Union

- 119 -

I came to poetry late in life.

I wanted too many answers for that. I craved explanations and strategies. I needed control.

When my heart finally broke and the struggle to clamber out of the pit ceased, I was spent.

Then one day I re-read Hafiz, who said, somewhere,

> The heart is like that:
> blessed and ruined
> once it has known
> divine beauty.

And it made perfect sense.

A warmth flooded the darkness and the ancient words of the Psalm crept in through the ruins and made new promises.

> Where can I go from your spirit?
> Or where can I flee from your presence?
> If I ascend to heaven, you are there;
> if I make my bed in Sheol, you are there.

The darkness itself became home.

> If I say, 'Surely the darkness shall cover me,

and the light around me become night',
even the darkness is not dark to you;
the night is as bright as the day,
for darkness is as light to you.

Incense billowed from ash-pits and the scattered, smouldering fires turned the rubble into holy ground.

I was surrounded by altars. Everything was an altar.

Time to take the shoes off, he said, when I told him.

- 120 -

There comes a time for silence.

The proverbs tell us that "even a fool, when he holds his peace, is counted wise: and he that shuts his lips is esteemed a man of understanding."

But that's not the kind of silence I am talking about. I am talking about a stuttering, speechless, awestruck kind of silence. It's a heartbroken silence because this love and this beauty undoes a man and leaves him awash with grateful tears.

Thomas Merton put it beautifully when he wrote about Pure Love in his Seeds of Contemplation. He said that "Here all adjectives fall to pieces. Words become stupid… Metaphor has now become hopeless altogether."

The best I could do was revert to biblical clichés and the words of those far more eloquent than me.

Thank God you've run out of things to say, he quipped.

I had to laugh. He had been very patient with me.

It was August and I was beginning to run out of money. I had found a tenant for Forge Lane and I was wondering where I was going to live next.

When do you have to move? he asked.

January, I answered.

Where will you go?

I don't know yet, I said. *There might be a job coming up.*

The Diocese were making noises about a position in a large, busy parish to the south.

Do you want it? he asked.

No, I said. *I don't think I do.*

I had got to the place where I couldn't see the point of it.

Everything good, from my initial conversion to the sporadic mystical experiences that graced my earlier Christian life, and the recent dissolution and reconstruction of my Christian faith at the hands of Harvey, had all happened outside the Church.

I didn't think, in good conscience, that I could recommend her to anyone.

How, if that were the case, could I work for her? She deserves people who believe in her.

Part 5: Dismissal

And why do you worry about clothing? Consider the lilies of the field, how they grow; they neither toil nor spin, yet I tell you, even Solomon in all his glory was not clothed like one of these. But if God so clothes the grass of the field, which is alive today and tomorrow is thrown into the oven, will he not much more clothe you—you of little faith?

Matthew 6:28-30

- 121 -

It was early autumn.

We were sitting outside at the Crab Apple Café waiting for food.

Tell me about your churches again, he said.

Again? I asked.

I had been through my progress through the Christian denominations with him before.

He always laughed when I described it as progress.

Well, I replied, *it started off Roman Catholic when I was a baby and up until I left school.*

He nodded.

Then, after That Night, when God became real, I ended up in a Charismatic House Church.[61]

Know what they are? I asked.

Yes, he said. *How was that?*

The waitress brought our food and he asked for ketchup.

It was good to begin with, I said, *But I couldn't cope for long.*

He laughed when I said that.

It's a lot of hard work, being saved by the blood, isn't it?

I had to think about that for a second. He had a wry smile on his face as he watched and waited for my reaction.

It was exhausting, I admitted.

I had to laugh.

And now? he asked.

I'm an Anglican, I said. *By the skin of my teeth.*

Ah, yes, he nodded. *Of course, you are.*

He was savouring his food as he spoke.

What do you mean by that? I asked.

Just that, now you mention it, I remember you telling me that a while ago, he replied.

He finished chewing another mouthful and asked, *What did you think I meant by that?*

It took a moment before I said, *Something along the lines of it being the least toxic church available.*

He finished off his plate in silence and then said, *So now you know why you're there.*

He put his knife and fork together on the plate, wiped his mouth with the napkin and asked, *Can I have one of your cigarettes?*

Sure, I said. *Help yourself.*

Thanks, he said. *Sometimes, I love a smoke after lunch, and this is one of those days.*

Later, after coffee, he finished me off: *Have you noticed something?* he asked.

What? I said.

How spiritually promiscuous you are?

He chuckled to himself.

You've been looking for a chance to deliver that line, I said.

He laughed and nodded.

I have, he said.

- 122 -

By the beginning of October, he was visibly thinner.

His skin was pale. It reminded me of baking paper.

He was translucent. Fading.

It was as though that fragile flesh could no longer carry those searing silver-blue eyes.

- 123 -

Words have started flowing, thick and fast, I said. *Phrases and sentences too.*

Is that a recent thing? he asked.

It's always been like this, from time to time. Since I was in my teens, I replied.

We were in town, walking uphill. The high street was full of people.

I had taken the length of hazel he had harvested and fashioned a thumb-stick for him. He called it his crook and teased me: *You're trying to turn me into a bishop!*

It reached to about shoulder-level and he could rest on it by leaning into a V-shaped groove at the top end.

There are times, like seasons, when I can't catch them, though, I continued.

We walked past the post office and he tossed a couple of coins into the busker's violin case.

As though they're falling leaves in a wind. And my hands are too big. Too slow and clumsy.

We stepped off the pavement and on to the road to avoid a crowd of teenagers on their way home from school.

Sometimes they flit by and I catch them for a moment, but they slip out of my grasp and I forget them. Other times they settle and stay but I have to wrestle them into shape until they become something.

Like Jacob wrestling the angel? He was listening to me intently.

And sometimes, they're so heavy I think I might break, I said.

We got to the top of the high street and stood for a while. He leant against the staff for support. He was tired.

Reminds me of the Parables, he said.

How? I asked.

Well, he said, *they're not really for reading.*

He turned to look back down the High Street. It was a beautiful, sunny day and the paddocks beyond were peppered with sheep.

No, I replied. *They're not.*

They're more like anvils than stories.

He laughed.

Part 5: Dismissal

Yes. He nodded. *They are anvils. Of course, they are.*

He walked on.

Maybe you can write that, one day?

Maybe, I replied.

- 124 -

As summer turned to autumn, I watched the world and the time go by, walked the dog, and wondered where I'd be in a few months.

My year in Forge Lane hadn't amounted to much at all. I had achieved nothing and that was the hardest part of it all for a while. All I'd done is survive and, looking back on the darkness and horror of it all, I can't begin to explain how I did that. I put one foot in front of the other, moment by moment.

My old Bishop retired to a great demonstration of love and appreciation. He was well-loved, the old man, and rightly so.

The Archdeacon was appointed bishop of a diocese in the south-east. That didn't surprise anyone. I never liked him, so it put a smile on my face to remember that W. H. Vanstone was convinced that bishops were either stupid or vain, or in some instances both.

It did seem that the best ones, like my old Bishop, were the ones who had never coveted the post.

Anyway, the Archdeacon asked me to write an autobiographical article about myself for the diocesan magazine before he left. I think he thought that he had managed me back into the fold and this was his attempt to publicise his pastoral prowess.

I always felt like a minor character in his ministry show.

I couldn't resist pissing on his parade, so, this is what I wrote:

> I don't much like the Church.
>
> It's a relief, after thirty-odd years of trying, to admit to that troubling fact and decide that she's probably just not the one for me.
>
> A horror of divorce lurks deep in the bones of this cradle Catholic, so it wasn't the easiest of decisions.
>
> Truth be told it wasn't a decision at all, in the ordinary sense of that word: I just woke up one Sunday morning and couldn't face her. The months have gone by and I am not at all sure that I will ever face her again.
>
> The air is far sweeter out here. It's pregnant with the heady scents of relief and freedom and faith. The Scriptures still sing their impossible promises and the Spirit still hovers over the waters giving life to the dead and calling into existence the things that do not exist as though they do (see Romans 4:17).

Elizabeth Barret Browning wrote that:

Earth's crammed with heaven,
And every common bush afire with God,
But only he who sees takes off his shoes;
The rest sit round and pluck blackberries.[62]

Moses knew that (Exodus 3:1-3).

So, I realised something, perhaps for the first time, though it was something I glimpsed in waves for many years: I actually believe the Gospel.

Actually, it's better than that: I know it's true.

And I know, beyond all shadow of doubt, that it's not conditional on church membership of any kind. When he suffered outside the gate, it wasn't only for the people left inside the gate (Hebrews 13:12).

The Church does such a good job of subtly telling people she's indispensable for their salvation, as though God is somehow her possession to give away only to her members. Churches may deny it and point to official statements to the contrary but anyone with any in-depth experience of church life and culture will admit to an insidious, and often unconscious conviction, that salvation is not by faith at all: it's by church membership.

It's time that credible voices (and I know there are many) spoke for salvation outside the Church.

My experience doesn't begin and end with the Catholic Church: there was a ten-year spell in an Evangelical, Charismatic House Church in London, a degree in theology at a Catholic college and, eventually, ordination in the Anglican Church.

I suppose they all served their purpose (dare I say they all brought me to this place in their own way?) but I can't shake the feeling, well and truly settled now, that promising so much, they are all so disappointing.

I wonder why I bothered for so long?

One night, in the early 1980s, God came into my life like a flood from which I, happily, never recovered. I was born-again in the most classic sense of that word and invaded with a love so overwhelming, so unconditional, that I still can't put it into words adequately. It's a common experience judging from ongoing research by bodies like the Alister Hardy Religious Experience Research Centre.

It wasn't until I wandered into a church voluntarily for the first time, seeking membership, that my re-education in a curriculum of conditional love began in earnest. It's a deeply cherished agenda and a powerful one at that.

My evangelical friends would often talk about God's restorative power and quote a much-loved scripture: "I will repay you for the years the locusts have eaten" (Joel 2:25). It's an irony that those locusts were buzzing around happily enough in the culture of the church we attended and that many of us are now applying that scripture to the years the church stole from us.

The voice that whispers, without respite, that we are not quite right with God unless...or until...is a compelling one and it's one I came to believe. It was a betrayal of that initial demonstration of God's love and I am still a bit puzzled by why I bought into it so enthusiastically.

No matter. I am happy out here, bare footing it around the common bushes, for now.

It was never published, and I never heard from the Archdeacon again.

That was the point.

- 125 -

That night I had my last dream about my old Bishop.

He was not in clerical dress. He was in hiking boots with an old Barbour coat and a flat-cap.

He carried Harvey's staff.

We were walking together across what looked like a beautiful moorland. There were tors of granite rock here and there. Wild ponies roamed free. It reminded me of Dartmoor.

Philo walked alongside me, and the bishop had a dog with him. She was a beautiful, young springer spaniel who kept trying to provoke a lazy Philo into play.

I read your article, he said.

Oh? I answered. *How did you get hold of that?*

Never mind, he said.

We walked on. I felt apprehensive as I waited for his comments.

What did you think? I asked.

He didn't answer immediately.

Some twenty or thirty paces on all he said was: *I thought it was pretentious. The noisy gonging of the clanging cymbals is still ringing in my ears.*

Shit! I exclaimed. *That doesn't sound good.*

No. He shook his head. *Not at all.*

I knew the old man was made of steel when he needed to be, but I had never experienced that aspect of him when it was unsheathed and pointing at me. Perhaps he had indulged me.

It made me wonder why you find it so difficult to love us, he continued.

It was something I had thought about myself.

There's a well-worn phrase in some circles that goes something like this: If you think you are enlightened, spend some time with your family.

It's easy to talk the talk from a distance but there's something about being enmeshed in an intimate community that has a way of finding us out.

What I think is that you still need to decide on something, he continued.

And what's that? I asked.

He looked at me then, with a warm smile on his face.

You need to decide who you are going to love, he said.

I didn't reply.

Your new robes might get torn and soiled when you do, he continued. *Loving is always a messy business.*

I was feeling uncomfortable. This wasn't his usual supportive, paternal approach.

We walked on in silence and I noticed that a light rain was falling.

A line from G. K. Chesterton came to mind. He said that Christians needed to find a way of loving the world without trusting it; without being worldly, and I wondered whether it was possible to find a way of loving the Church without trusting her; without being churchly.[63]

I'm still wondering.

I think we can agree on one thing, he said, after what seemed like a long time.

Oh? I was relieved that some kind of lighter conversation might begin to flow.

Well, he said, *I don't think you'll ever make bishop.*

He turned to the left abruptly, called on his dog to follow him and said, over his shoulder, *Come on. This way. I'll buy you a pint.*

- 126 -

Harvey made apple and blackberry crumble for us one afternoon, after a long, slow walk.

He wanted to see the autumn flowering of the wild cyclamen that was on display under the big cedar trees on the higher ground above the water meadows. The pink flames were still in bloom, reaching up through the dark foliage like little crowns on stalks.

It was worth the trip, but he was struggling.

Later, we sipped tea at his kitchen table while we waited for the oven to do its work.

I don't know what it is that survived the fire, I said. *I know it's me, but somehow, it's not me.*

He was nodding.

It's the great question, he said. *And the great answer, too.* He smiled.

What is? I asked.

What is it that survives the tribulation? he answered.[64]

Yes, that's it, I said.

How is it that I am here, when what I thought was me is no longer intact?

It can't be named, he said. *It just is, that's all.*

He was right, of course, but my heart was too full to let it lie.

I can't resist a Meister Eckhart quote, I said.[65]

Oh? That intellectual face is still around, is it? he asked.

When it feels like it, I answered. *From time to time.*

Go on then, he sighed. *For the last time.*

Here goes. I winked at him while he waited.

"What does God do all day long? He gives birth. From the beginning of eternity, God lies on a maternity bed giving birth to all. God is creating this whole universe full and entire in this present moment."

I like that, he said.

He pulled the crumble from the oven and laid it on the countertop.

Smells good, he said. *Can you get plates out?*

It was good. The tart Bramley apples, blackberries, and dark brown sugar were made for each other.

Got any ice cream? I asked.

Vanilla in the freezer, he said.

We ate in silence for a while.

The peace was thick and sweet, and I was filled with an overwhelming sense of gratitude for his presence in my life. He was the closest thing to a father I had ever known.

There's a beautiful Sufi story, he said. *You might understand it now.*

Tell it to me, I said.

A man went to the door of the Beloved and knocked. A voice asked: "Who is there?" He answered: "It is I." The voice said: "There is no room here for me and thee." The door was shut.

I was watching him as he spoke. His eyes shone. *After a year of solitude and deprivation this man returned to the door of the Beloved.*

A beautiful smile played across his lips as he searched for, and remembered, the words. *He knocked. A voice from within asked: "Who is there?" The man said: "It is Thou."*[66]

He paused then, looked me straight in the eye and said, *The door was opened for him.*

It seemed to sum up what I was feeling perfectly but I couldn't resist a quip. *Did you ever take that man to the pub?* I asked.

He smiled and answered, quite casually, *No. He was far more serious about it all than you were. He never wasted his time in the pub.*

I laughed at that.

Then he said, *He didn't know what he was missing, the poor fool!*

- 127 -

Looking back on the time I spent with him, I find it difficult to explain how it was that he helped me, because he didn't really help at all in the conventional sense of that word.

God had hold of me like a lion his prey and Harvey didn't do much more than sit back and watch it happen. There was no sense, ever, that he was going to be the one to snatch me from the jaws of death.

Let yourself burn, he said. *There's nothing else you can do.*

There really wasn't much more to it than that.

Let yourself burn? There's more to that little line than meets the eye.

A celebrated Orthodox nun, Mother Maria Skobtsova, once wrote in wartime Paris: "Either Christianity is fire, or there is no such thing."[67]

Did he minister to me? Not in the traditional sense. Did he intercede for me? Never that I knew of. Did he care for me? Not in the conventional manner.

He never allowed himself to believe any of my stories. He wasn't convinced by my version of my so-called self.

Why are you hoping that I will be nicer to you than God? he would ask. *If God has thrown you in a pit, what makes you think I have any interest in lifting you out of it?*

Today I often wonder how many ministers would be content to sit and watch a person burn, as he did. I've never met one. Most seem to be in the business of saving us from God.

Harvey was the furthest thing from a professional saviour that I have ever met.

I'm just the witness, he would often say. *That's all. The work is God's, not mine.*

Part 5: Dismissal

What I do know is that his description of himself as a midwife rang true. He accompanied me. He challenged me. He destroyed me. He encouraged me.

He was my only friend apart from Philo.

- 128 -

At some point, early in the autumn of our second year, I realised I was seeing less of him.

What struck me when I thought it over, was my own, quite comfortable, resignation to that fact. He had told me that my loneliness would flower into solitude at some stage and time was proving him right. In my own isolation, I had discovered the enduring companionship that Harvey had promised and pointed to.

e. e. cummings put it better than most ever could.

>   no time ago
>   or else a life
>   walking in the dark
>   i met christ
>
>   Jesus) my heart
>   flopped over
>   and lay still
>   while He passed (as

close as i'm to you
yes closer
made of nothing
except loneliness[68]

You knew I'd find him there, didn't you? I asked when I did see him.

Yes, he said. *You and everyone else who could ever bear to look. You're not that special.*

That made me smile.

There was a time I would have been offended by his constant need to burst the bubble of my narcissism, but I had become more than grateful for it. It was his job, and I was beginning to realise how good he was at it.

Faithful are the wounds of a friend, I said.

He nodded and said, *I love that proverb.*

Pint? I asked.

Why not, he said.

As we walked the familiar steps from his place to the pub, I noticed that we walked in time.

My heart was full.

Part 5: Dismissal

- 129 -

Have you written anything lately?

It was unlike him to ask.

I was normally the one who pressed my writing on him. I was looking for confirmation that I had realised the truths he had been trying to teach me. I was also looking for approval.

But by the end of that autumn, I no longer needed either.

By the end of that autumn, I wasn't seeing him because I wasn't looking for anything anymore. I was no longer seeking. I was no longer in pain. I was seeing him because I knew that our time was running out and I wanted to make the most of him.

I have, I nodded. *Yes.*

Do you want me to show you some of it?

No, he said. He held his hand up.

But I'd like you to read me some if you have something with you.

He leant back in his reclining chair and closed his eyes.

This one's still a work in progress, I said. *But I think I like it.*

He nodded.

*It was only after I had gone that all
Your love songs came, pouring their
never-ending promises through the
narrow gate like a pack of playful dogs.*

*A hundred thousand eager voices,
ever ancient, ever new, lifted their
veils and vowed, by their secret Name,
that nothing lost will not be found.*

*For better, for worse, all that is must
pass away this way, into this warm sea
of singing reeds, of infinitely patient arms
and under the chorus of these caresses.*

His fire was burning in the grate. Philo was curled up next to it. I was on his sofa.

At last! he said, smiling. *You're not in it.*

His eyes were still closed.

Perfect, he said, before he fell soundly asleep.

I wrapped a blanket around him, put another log on the fire, put a lead on Philo and left, quietly.

Part 5: Dismissal

- 130 -

The last time I saw him was late November.

We were at the pub. We drank a strong autumn ale and basked in the glow of a roaring fire. It was bitterly cold. The icy Siberian winds were relentless. Philo lay in a circle of dogs by the fire and we talked and drank.

We stayed until the early hours of the morning.

As we sat, watching the fire's graceful flames, Harvey recited from the Song of Solomon, quietly.

> *"Set me as a seal upon your heart,*
> *as a seal upon your arm;*
> *for love is strong as death,*
> *passion fierce as the grave.*
> *Its flashes are flashes of fire,*
> *a raging flame.*
> *Many waters cannot quench love,*
> *neither can floods drown it."*

He was saying goodbye.

The words swam through me and I heard them, deep in the marrow of my bones, as if for the first time.

But you know all that now, don't you? he asked.

I nodded. I knew.

He stayed at mine, in Forge Lane, that night. It was far too cold to brave the walk to his place.

In the morning, when I woke and came down to make coffee, he was gone. The pillow and blanket were still sprawled across my sofa. Philo had installed himself in the residual warmth of his body. He didn't move when I called him.

I smoked out in the garden as I drank the coffee. The weather had turned overnight, and the wind had stilled. It was warmer outside.

- 131 -

And it struck me in his absence: the Christ and the Apostles, they have not deceived me.

- 132 -

I dreamt of him, repeatedly, over the next few weeks. Just his wrinkled, smiling face and those piercing, childlike eyes. He looked like a psalm. Brim-full, pressed down and running over with the strangest, fiercest joy I have ever seen.

Part 5: Dismissal

It was as though he couldn't take his eyes off me. I could smell him too.

He only spoke in one of the dreams. It was pure mischief.

I've prayed for you, he said.

Thank you, I answered.

We were walking in the water-meadows. Philo was with us, along with another dog; a beautiful, young, female springer spaniel.

I've made God promise me something, he added.

Oh? I asked.

That he would never answer any of your prayers your way.

Then he was gone, along with the dog.

All that was left was Philo, the sound of his laughter and the bubbling whisper of the stream.

- 133 -

I walked Philo up to his place just before Christmas.

It reminded me of the day we first met, and I half-expected him to appear from behind a hawthorn hedge at any moment. The whole place seemed alive with him.

The autumn leaves had given way to stark, silver-black lines and the breeze bit.

I strolled, happily enough, behind Philo, who headed for the path to his house.

It was empty.

A 'TO LET' sign stood meters from the front door, which was open.

Can I take a look? I asked the agent.

Sure, he shrugged. *I'll leave you to it.*

He was measuring the kitchen, pad in hand.

Philo settled by the cold fireplace and I headed down the corridor to his bedroom. I had never seen it.

The oak floor was marked, in places, so I noticed where a bed and solitary chest of drawers would have sat. It had a deep, ingrained smell of wood smoke.

To the right, a large sash window looked out onto the empty fields.

To the left, a door led me into a bathroom. It was almost as big as the bedroom, with a huge cast-iron bath that must have been installed when the place was built. Another large window overlooked the garden.

I turned and caught my reflection in the mirror before noticing in it, a note, pinned on the door of a large, built-in airing cupboard behind me.

It was in his handwriting and the note read: "Right place. Right time. Wrong clothes."[69]

I opened the cupboard.

My vestments were neatly arranged on hangers, inside.

Take down the sign, I said to the agent on the way out.

Philo followed quietly.

I'll take it.

Epilogue

There's nothing left to
do now but peel your
shredded clothes off.

Then step that final
step into the pages
of the burning book.

This fire, that calls the
empty faces You have
worn in me, home again.

The truth is that you
are a secret that is best
kept from yourself.

Endnotes

The structure of this book follows the order of the Mass, where people gather (Assembly); confess and receive absolution (Purification); listen to readings and a sermon (Illumination); take communion (Union); and are, finally, sent on their way (Dismissal).

Bible quotes are from the New Revised Standard Version (1989) Anglicised Edition with a couple of exceptions where the King James Version is used.

Part 1: Assembly

[1] Harvey is an English and Scottish name derived from a Breton origin. It means "battle worthy." St Harvey (Breton - Hervé) was born in Wales and died about AD 575. He became one of the most popular saints in Brittany. Being born blind, he is a patron of the eyes, illnesses of the eyes and blindness.

[2] The Eucharist (or Holy Communion) is the central Christian act of worship. It commemorates and represents the death and resurrection of Jesus.

The Alb is a white, long-sleeved garment that reaches down to the ankles. It is worn under other liturgical vestments (clothing worn during worship services) and symbolises purity.

The Stole is a long, usually silk, scarf of sorts. It is worn over the Alb and it is the symbol denoting those in Holy Orders.

The Chasuble is the outermost liturgical vestment, worn over the Alb and the Stole. It could plausibly be described as a kind of poncho. It symbolises the 'yoke' (or burden) of Christ and symbolises charity or love.

3 The goal of the mystical life may be said to be Union with God. Ecstatic Union refers to the sense, often imparted during an ecstatic religious experience, of oneness with the divine. Habitual union refers to an ongoing consciousness of oneness with God which persists as one lives the ordinary round of daily life.

4 Three well-known Christian Spiritual practices. Lectio Divina is a prayerful, meditative reading of Scripture. Centering Prayer is an apparently ancient mantra-based meditative practice adapted for modern times by Fathers Thomas Keating, William Meninger and Basil Pennington. The Daniel Fast (especially popular with North American Protestants) involves eating only fruits, vegetables, legumes, whole grains, nuts, and seeds; avoiding "choice foods" such as meat, dairy, and sugars; and drinking only water.

5 The Phantom is an image taken from Thomas Merton's Conjectures Of A Guilty Bystander in which he quotes Father Paul

Evdokimov, "One goes into the desert to vomit up the interior phantom, the doubter, the double." It's a more poetic way of talking about the false self or the ego.

[6] Hebrew 'tefillin.' In Jewish religious practice the word denotes either of two small square leather boxes containing slips inscribed with scriptural passages and traditionally worn on the left arm and on the head by observant Jewish men. Jesus mentions phylacteries when he criticises the Pharisees for their love of conspicuous shows of spirituality: "They do all their deeds to be seen by others; for they make their phylacteries broad and their fringes long." (Matthew 23:5)

[7] William (Bill) Hubert Vanstone (1923–1999) was a Church of England priest. He seemed set for a glittering academic career but chose, instead, to serve as a simple parish priest, as well as writing a number of small spiritual books, hymns, and verses. *The Stature of Waiting* and *Love's Endeavour, Love's Expense* are two of the better-known ones. The reference is to *The Stature of Waiting*.

[8] *It Is Well With My Soul* (1876, by Horatio Spafford and composed by Philip Bliss) was written after traumatic events in Spafford's life. The first two were the death of his four-year-old son and the Great Chicago Fire of 1871, which ruined him financially. He was further affected by the economic downturn of 1873, at which time he had planned to travel to Europe with his family on the SS. Ville du Havre. In a late change of plan, he sent

the family ahead while he was delayed on business. While crossing the Atlantic, the ship sank after colliding with a sea vessel, the Loch Earn, and all four of Spafford's daughters died. His wife Anna survived and sent him the now famous telegram, "*Saved alone...*" Shortly afterwards, as Spafford travelled to meet his wife, he was inspired to write these words as his ship passed near where his daughters had died. Bliss called his tune Ville du Havre, from the name of the sunken vessel.

[9] George Fox (1624–1691) was an English Dissenter, who was a founder of the Religious Society of Friends, commonly known as the Quakers or Friends. Fox's journal was first published in 1694. In Chapter 1 he writes: "As I thus travelled through the country, professors took notice of me, and sought to be acquainted with me; but I was afraid of them, for I was sensible they did not possess what they professed."

[10] A reference to the well-known and well-loved Parable of the Prodigal Son in Luke's Gospel (Luke 15:11-32).

[11] Thomas Merton OCSO (1915–1968) was an American Trappist monk, writer, theologian, mystic, poet, social activist, and scholar of comparative religion. The quote comes from his celebrated autobiography *The Seven Storey Mountain* (1948).

Endnotes

Part 2: Purification

[12] *The Hound of Heaven* is a poem by Francis Thompson (1859–1907). He was an opium addict and street vagrant for years before he was discovered, and his first set of poems were published in 1893.

[13] Friedrich Nietzsche (1844–1900) was a German philosopher, cultural critic, composer, poet, and philologist. The son of a Lutheran pastor, Nietzsche himself began the study of theology and classical philology at the University of Bonn with the intention of becoming a minister. He lasted one semester before losing his faith. Nietzsche's searing and penetrative critiques of Christianity have had a profound effect. I have heard him referred to, ironically, as a 'Doctor of the Church' (a title given by the Catholic Church to saints recognised as having made a significant contribution to theology or doctrine through their thinking) in some quarters, along with Feuerbach, Freud, and others. The quote is taken from his *Human All Too Human 1.87.*

[14] John Steinbeck (1902–1968) was an American author. He won the 1962 Nobel Prize in Literature and many of his works are considered classics of Western literature. The book referred to here is *The Log from the Sea of Cortez.*

15 Albert Camus (1913–1960) was a French existential philosopher, author, and journalist. He won the Nobel Prize in Literature at the age of 44.

16 Teresa of Ávila (1515–1582) was a Spanish Carmelite nun, mystic, religious reformer, author, and theologian of the contemplative life. She was declared Doctor of the Church over four centuries after her death. She reformed the Carmelite Orders of both women and men and her new movement (the Discalced Carmelites) was later joined by the younger Spanish Carmelite friar and mystic, John of the Cross.

17 Jean-Paul Sartre (1905–1980) was a French philosopher, playwright, novelist, screenwriter, political activist, biographer, and literary critic. He was a key figure in the philosophy of existentialism and phenomenology, and one of the leading figures in 20th-century French philosophy and Marxism. The quote is from *The Words* (1964).

18 Socrates (c. 470–399 BC) was an early and very influential Greek Philosopher from Athens who influenced Plato and thereby set the course for the entire western philosophical tradition. He was famous for his 'Socratic Method' of rigorous and ruthless questioning in the pursuit of fundamental truths, especially when it came to issues of justice and goodness. He was referred to as a "gadfly" because, as a gadfly stings a horse, so Socrates 'stung' various powerful, high ranking Athenians. This eventually led to his death.

[19] In Hebrew thought, Sheol is a place of darkness to which the dead go. Those in Sheol are the 'shades' (Rephaim), entities without personality or strength.

[20] Gerard Manley Hopkins SJ (1844–1889) was an English poet, Catholic convert and Jesuit priest, whose posthumous fame established him among the leading Victorian poets. The quote is from Sonnet 65 of his *Terrible Sonnets*.

[21] St John Climacus, also known as John of the Ladder, John Scholasticus and John Sinaites, was a 6th-7th-century Christian monk at the monastery on Mount Sinai. He is revered as a saint by the Roman Catholic, Eastern Orthodox and Eastern Catholic churches.

[22] See Matthew 22:36-40, where Jesus is cross-examined by a group of religious professionals: "Teacher, which commandment in the law is the greatest?" He said to him, "'You shall love the Lord your God with all your heart, and with all your soul, and with all your mind.' This is the greatest and first commandment. And a second is like it: 'You shall love your neighbour as yourself.' On these two commandments hang all the law and the prophets." Most Christians will accept the Greatest Commandment as the core of Christian practice.

[23] For "the kernel stays in the grave," see John 12:24-25 where Jesus says: "Very truly, I tell you, unless a grain of wheat falls into the earth and dies, it remains just a single grain; but if it dies, it bears much fruit. Those who love their life lose it, and those who

hate their life in this world will keep it for eternal life."

24 For "the branches stay in the fire. Only the vine emerges," see John 15:5-6 where Jesus says: "I am the vine, you are the branches. Those who abide in me and I in them bear much fruit, because apart from me you can do nothing. Whoever does not abide in me is thrown away like a branch and withers; such branches are gathered, thrown into the fire, and burned."

25 For "only the First-Born opens death's womb," see Colossians 1:15-18 where St Paul writes: "He is the image of the invisible God, the firstborn of all creation; for in him all things in heaven and on earth were created, things visible and invisible, whether thrones or dominions or rulers or powers—all things have been created through him and for him. He himself is before all things, and in him all things hold together. He is the head of the body, the church; he is the beginning, the firstborn from the dead, so that he might come to have first place in everything."

26 The Cell of Self-Knowledge is a phrase attributed to Catherine of Siena (1347–1380) and used as the title of a book, *The cell of self-knowledge: seven early English mystical treatises,* printed by Henry Pepwell in 1521.

27 St Thérèse of Lisieux (1873–1897) was a French Catholic Discalced Carmelite nun who is widely venerated in modern times. Thérèse has been a very influential model of sanctity for Catholics and for others because of the simplicity and practicality of her approach to the spiritual life. She became a nun at the age

of 15 and describes the last period of her life as a 'night of faith' (a time when she felt Jesus was absent and when she felt tormented by doubts about the existence of God). Thérèse died at the age of 24, from tuberculosis. The quote is taken from a letter to her sister.

Part 3: Illumination

[28] Old Nick is an old English nickname for Satan.

[29] The waters of Baptism have long been compared tomb and a womb. See Cyril of Jerusalem's *Catechetical Lecture 20 (On The Mysteries. Ii.4) Of Baptism*: "And At The Self-same moment you were both dying and being born; and that Water of salvation was at once your grave and your mother."

[30] St John of the Cross (1542–1591) was a Carmelite friar, priest, mystic, poet, and theologian. He is universally recognised as one of the greatest mystical writers of all time. His celebrated *Dark Night of the Soul* and the *Ascent of Mount Carmel* are considered the pinnacle of mystical theology in the Catholic tradition.

[31] Gregory Zilboorg (1890–1959) was a Ukrainian psychoanalyst and historian of psychiatry. He was raised as an Orthodox Jew but abandoned his ancestral faith in his 20s. When the Bolsheviks took over, he fled to Holland, then to the United States in 1919.

He converted to Catholicism in 1945.

32 A Fresh Expression of church is a form of church established primarily for the benefit of people who are not yet members of any church. They are self-consciously different in ethos and style from the church which planted them. So, there are so-called churches in pubs and skateboard parks, artists' studios, and university student unions.

33 Hafiz or Hafez (Khwāja Shams-ud-Dīn Muḥammad Ḥāfeẓ-e Shīrāzī 1315–1390) was a Persian Sufi poet. He celebrated the joys of divine love but also targeted religious hypocrisy. His collected works are regarded as a pinnacle of Persian literature.

34 The quote is taken from *The Gift: Poems by Hafiz, the Great Sufi Master. Translated by Daniel Ladinsky.* These are not really translations from the original Persian—they are rather to be understood as Ladinsky's own mystical poetry, perhaps inspired by his reading of the great Sufi poet.

35 For the wonderfully entertaining story of Samson, who ends up blinded and tied to a pillar in the temple of Dagon before collapsing the entire structure with his bare hands, read the *Book of Judges*, chapters 13-18.

36 Touch not the Lord's anointed is a phrase often used by Christian leaders, especially in Evangelical churches, to frighten their members into obedience. It is found in a variety of scripture texts, like Psalm 105:15 and 1 Chronicles 16:22. The irony, of

course, is that the greatest moment in salvation history came about precisely because God's anointed One was touched.

37 The Eastern Orthodox Church has traditionally understood the tree of life in Genesis as a prefiguration of the Cross, which bears the fruit that humanity can freely partake of after the death, resurrection, and ascension of Jesus.

38 The traditional place of Jesus' crucifixion and death. Golgotha (Calvary in western, Latin Christianity) means the place of the skull. See Luke 23:33: "When they came to the place that is called The Skull, they crucified Jesus there with the criminals, one on his right and one on his left."

39 Catherine of Genoa (1447–1510) was an Italian Roman Catholic saint and mystic. She wanted to join a convent when she was 13 but was rejected on account of her youth. Later, after 10 years in a very unhappy marriage, she had a profound mystical experience during confession and dedicated her life to the care of the poor and the sick.

40 Homiletics is the art of writing and preaching sermons. In some Christian denominations the sermon is referred to as the homily.

41 The story of Legion is, perhaps, an account of Jesus' most dramatic exorcism. See the full account in Mark 5:1-20.

42 See the *Ascent of Mount Carmel* (Prologue 4).

43 British slang for "take your clothes off."

44 See the *Ascent of Mount Carmel* (Book 1, Chapter 13, Section 11).

45 Harry Williams (1919–2006) was a Church of England priest, monk, theologian and academic. He was chaplain of Westcott House, Cambridge and then Trinity College, Cambridge, where he was a fellow and lecturer and was later Dean of Trinity College Chapel. In 1972, he left academia and entered religious life as a monk with the Community of the Resurrection. His autobiography, from which the quote comes, is called *Someday I'll Find You*.

Part 4: Union

46 Rufus Jones (1863–1948) was an American religious leader, writer, magazine editor, philosopher, and college professor. A historian and theologian as well as a philosopher, he was one of the most influential Quakers of the 20th century.

47 The German philosopher Immanuel Kant (1724–1804) was among the most influential of all time. His contribution, especially in his celebrated *Critique of Pure Reason*, has influenced areas of philosophy as diverse as epistemology, metaphysics, ethics, and aesthetics.

[48] The Desert Fathers (and Mothers) were Christian hermits, ascetics, and monks who lived mainly in the Scetes desert of Egypt around the third century AD. The most well-known was St Anthony the Great (251–356). By the time Anthony died, thousands of monks and nuns had been drawn to living in the desert following his example. The story is taken from *The Sayings of the Desert Fathers (Apophthegmata Patrum)*.

[49] A milksop is a weak, cowardly, ineffectual man. In the sense used here, this derogatory term signifies a certain spiritual immaturity. Milksops were pieces of bread soaked (sopped) in warm milk and often sweetened with sugar. The word is first attested to in 14th century England where milksops were given to infants, the infirm and elderly. It clearly has earlier roots, though; St Paul, writing to the Corinthians in the 1st century, has a similar criticism of those who chase after spiritual comforts rather than the more challenging diet of spiritual truths, which are often difficult to digest: "And so, brothers and sisters, I could not speak to you as spiritual people, but rather as people of the flesh, as infants in Christ. I fed you with milk, not solid food, for you were not ready for solid food. Even now you are still not ready." (1 Corinthians 3:1-2).

[50] For "judgement and love are not reconciled; neither does the lion lie with the lamb," see Isaiah, chapter 11 (especially verses 6-9), where a future Messianic kingdom is envisaged, in which all enemies become friends and all opposites are reconciled.

51 Augustine of Hippo (354–430) was a theologian, philosopher, and the bishop of Hippo in Roman North Africa. His writings influenced the development of Western philosophy and Christianity. This quote is from his celebrated autobiography, *Confessions* (3.6.11).

52 The Real Presence of Christ in the Eucharist is a term used in Christian, especially Catholic, theology to express the doctrine that Jesus is really or substantially present in the Eucharist, not merely symbolically or metaphorically.

53 A "lock-in" is when a pub owner lets drinkers stay in the pub after the legal closing time. The idea is that once the doors are locked, it becomes a private party rather than a pub.

54 *St Patrick's Breastplate* is a prayer attributed to Ireland's patron saint. According to tradition, St Patrick wrote it in AD 433 for divine protection before successfully converting the Irish King Leoghaire and his subjects from paganism to Christianity. The term breastplate refers to a piece of armour worn in battle.

55 The "Manna" was a mythical, heavenly food provided by God to the Israelites as they wandered for 40 years in the desert. It is described in Exodus 16:1-36 and Numbers 11:7-9 as being a fine, flake-like substance like the frost on the ground. The Israelites ground it and baked it, resulting in something that tasted like honey-cakes baked with oil.

56 Saint Francis of Assisi was an Italian Catholic friar, deacon,

mystic, and preacher. He founded the Franciscans. Francis is one of the most venerated religious figures in Christianity and is best known for his radical, joyful poverty as well as his love for the natural world.

[57] Basil the Blessed was originally an apprentice shoemaker in Moscow. He adopted an eccentric lifestyle of shoplifting and giving to the poor to shame the miserly and help those in need. He went naked and weighed himself down with chains.

[58] British slang for a drunk.

[59] To be "hoist with your own petard" is to be blown up by your own bomb. Petard is a French name for a small, grenade-like explosive. The saying goes back to Shakespeare's *Hamlet*, Act 3, Scene 4. It has come to be used of any plot that ends up backfiring on the schemer. See also the bible on this: "Whoever digs a pit will fall into it, and a stone will come back on the one who starts it rolling." (Proverbs 26:27)

[60] Felix culpa is a Latin phrase that comes from the words felix, meaning happy and culpa, meaning fault. It comes from the Catholic hymn, the *Exsultet*, a long proclamation sung before the paschal candle during the Easter Vigil in the Roman Rite of the Mass. It is also used in Anglican and various Lutheran churches, as well as other Western Christian denominations. The lines referred to are: "O truly necessary sin of Adam, destroyed completely by the Death of Christ! O happy fault that earned for

us so great, so glorious a Redeemer!"

Part 5: Dismissal

[61] The Charismatic movement in Christianity is characterised by beliefs and practices similar to Pentecostalism, even though the movement is found within other denominations and in non-denominational communities. Fundamental to the movement is the experience of the baptism in the Holy Spirit and speaking in tongues (glossolalia) and the use of supernatural gifts. In the UK, some of these charismatic churches grew from small communities which initially met in each other's houses and so came to be called House Churches even after they migrated to larger venues.

[62] Elizabeth Barrett Browning (1806–1861) was an English Victorian poet. She was popular in Britain and the United States during her lifetime and her work had a major influence on prominent writers of the day, including the American poets Edgar Allan Poe and Emily Dickinson. Much of Barrett Browning's work deals with religious themes and her life was once described as a "Gospel of applied Christianity."

[63] G. K. Chesterton (1874–1936) was an English writer, philosopher, lay theologian, and literary and art critic. He routinely referred to himself as an "orthodox" Christian, and

came to identify this position more and more with Catholicism, eventually converting from High Church Anglicanism. The quote is taken from his apologetic book, *Orthodoxy* (1908).

[64] In Christian eschatology (teachings about the end times), the 'Great Tribulation' is a phrase used to describe a projected period of great suffering which will occur before the Second Coming of Jesus. Beliefs vary from denomination to denomination as is the case with much of Christian theology.

[65] Eckhart von Hochheim OP (1260–1328), commonly known as Meister Eckhart, was a German theologian, philosopher and mystic. His theology and teaching emphasised the presence of God in the human soul and the importance of the practice of detachment (letting go of one's 'self'). He was accused of and tried for heresy just before his death.

[66] This story is attributed to the great Persian Sufi poet and teacher Rumi (1207–1273). The story goes that he met a wandering teacher called Shams-e Tabrizi in 1244 and, such was the effect of this meeting, he turned his back on a promising career and became Shams' disciple until the latter's death in 1248. It was when Shams died that Rumi, grieving for his beloved master, realised union with God.

[67] Mother Maria Skobtsova was a Russian noblewoman, poet, nun, and member of the French Resistance during World War II. She has been canonised a saint in the Eastern Orthodox Church. She was sent to the Ravensbrück concentration camp. On Holy

Saturday, 1945, she died in a gas chamber.

[68] Edward Estlin "e. e." Cummings (1894–1962) was an American poet, painter, essayist, author, and playwright. His father was a Harvard Professor and Unitarian minister. His writing reflects a suspicion of established institutions and a conviction that organised religion was a failure. He is frequently quoted by people on non-traditional spiritual paths. The quote is *Untitled Poem 92*.

[69] For "Right place. Right time. Wrong clothes." see the Parable of the Wedding Banquet in Matthew Chapter 22. Especially verses 11–14: 'But when the king came in to see the guests, he noticed a man there who was not wearing a wedding robe, and he said to him, "Friend, how did you get in here without a wedding robe?" And he was speechless. Then the king said to the attendants, "Bind him hand and foot, and throw him into the outer darkness, where there will be weeping and gnashing of teeth." For many are called, but few are chosen.'

Acknowledgements

It seems to be standard practice among writers to acknowledge that there are too many people to acknowledge in a few hundred words. I'd like to add my name to that list and say that I think it's true. It's impossible to remember all those who, in some way, contributed to the story contained in these pages.

My thanks to all of them.

There are, however, some important folks to mention.

My thanks to Eva, my beautiful, brave, funny wife. She was among the first to read these words and she never stopped loving them and believing in them.

My thanks to Branka for the exquisite photograph on the front cover. She is one of my oldest, closest and dearest. She was also an early reader of the Naked Mystic and knows its landscapes intimately.

My thanks to Jody, my multi-talented, curious, adventurous friend.

My thanks to Sophie. She knows why.

My thanks to Richard Doyle, whose warm, humorous heart has enlivened this damp corner of England in these strange, isolated times. His wide-ranging erudition and playful eloquence make the Metanoia Press a vibrant, lively place in which to talk about that which cannot be talked about.

My thanks to Suzanne Winters at the Metanoia Press for making all this so easy.

Finally, my thanks to all those church-friends over all those years, but especially the good people of St Luke's, Mount Albert and All Saints, Howick in Auckland, New Zealand. Some of them read bits of this in its embryonic stages and made all the right noises. Without their grunts of approval, I might not be writing these words today.

About James R.Q. Clark

James RQ Clark is a former teacher and Anglican priest.

Born of a French-Mauritian mother and an English father who spent his working life roaming through Africa, the Middle and Far-East, James attended a Catholic Boarding school in the UK.

After a life-changing encounter with God in the early '80s and a stint in a British Charismatic Evangelical House Church, he reconnected with his Catholic roots and studied for his Theology degree at a Catholic college of the University of Surrey.

A journey through teaching and school chaplaincy led to his ordination in the Anglican Church of New Zealand in 2012.

These days he is settled in an old house, in an old town in Dorset, South-West England.

He walks his dogs, swims in the rivers, thinks, writes, and occasionally sees people for transpersonal counselling and spiritual direction (www.jamesrqclark.com).

Queries and responses welcome at jrqclark@gmail.com.

MetanoiaPress

Metanoia Press
www.metanoia.press

Printed in Great Britain
by Amazon